PEOPLE, LOVE, SEX, AND FAMILIES
Answers to Questions That Preteens Ask

Also by ERIC W. JOHNSON

PEOPLE, LOVE, SEX, AND FAMILIES
Answers to Questions That Preteens Ask

ERIC W. JOHNSON

ILLUSTRATIONS BY
DAVID WOOL

Walker and Company

New York

First published in the United States of America
in 1985 by the Walker Publishing Company, Inc.

Published simultaneously in Canada by Thomas Allen &
Son Canada, Limited, Markham, Ontario.

Library of Congress Cataloging-in-Publication Data
Johnson, Eric W.
  People, love, sex, and families.

  Includes index.
  Summary: Answers 200 questions posed by preteens about love, sex, reproduc-
tion, contraception, divorce, rape, child abuse, and other topics.
    1. Children's questions and answers—Juvenile
literature. [1. Sex instruction for children.
2. Conduct of life. 3. Questions and answers]
I. Wool, David, ill. II. Title.
HQ784.Q4J64 1985   306.7'07   85-15381
ISBN 0-8027-6591-2
ISBN 0-8027-6605-6 {Reinforced}
Printed in the United States of America

10 9 8 7 6 5 4 3

Contents

Note to Parents and Teachers

I'm sure that when many of you read this book you will be surprised—maybe even shocked—at the kinds of questions fourth-, fifth-, and sixth-graders ask, especially about sex. Some advance readers of the book wrote such comments as "You mean nine-year-olds are asking *that?*" or "I think this is way beyond what's really on these kid's minds."

My reply is that I was somewhat surprised too. But, yes, nine-year-olds (fourth-graders), as well as ten- and eleven-year-olds, *are* asking "that." And I've dealt only with questions that *several* boys and girls asked, not just one or two precocious ones. Furthermore, it can't be beyond what's on the kids' minds, because on my totally open-ended questionnaire (simply blank pages on which to write), these are the questions they asked, and this is the information they said they wanted. A couple of typical student comments are:

I really want to know all this, but nobody knows I do. If they knew, they'd kill me. So please keep it a secret, but write the book fast. I need to know.   —Fourth-grade boy.

WOW! That was embarrassing to ask all those questions. I never did before. PLEASE answer them as fast as possible. It may be too late.   —Fifth-grade girl.

If young people have heavy questions on their minds, they're going to try to get answers. It's better for them to have factual, well-balanced answers than answers based on ignorance, rumor, or partial information. Therefore, this book.

E. W. J.

— Introduction: —

Information, Please

For a long time, boys and girls in grades four, five, and six, have needed a book that would answer *their own* questions about people, love, sex, and families. It should tell them what they want to know, not just what adults think boys and girls want to know.

That's why I wrote this book. It is based on a confidential, open-ended questionnaire that simply said, "Please write on the next blank pages: (1) *facts* you want to know about people, love, sex, and families; (2) *questions* you want to ask." Then there were two blank lined pages on which to write. At the top of the first blank page was this box:

```
I am a boy (  ).
I am a girl (  ).
My age is _____.
My grade is _____.
```

About a thousand boys and girls filled out the questionnaires in their classrooms. They came from public, parochial, and independent schools. They came from families that range from poor to rich. Most came from cities and towns, some from country areas.

As soon as each questionnaire was finished, the student sealed it in an envelope and gave the sealed envelope to the teacher. All the envelopes were then returned directly to me. On the envelope was printed *QUESTIONNAIRE to be read only by Eric W. Johnson, 6110 Ardleigh St., Philadelphia, PA 19138.* Thus I am the only

1

person who has seen what the students wrote. Furthermore, except for the one school where I first tried out the questionnaire, I have no idea who wrote each reply or what school he or she came from.

Many students asked some questions that are so broad that even if I knew the answers I couldn't deal with them in a short book. Here are some examples:

What causes intelligence?
What is God? How did religion start?
Why are people mean?
What causes crime, poverty, and hatred?
Why do we have wars?
What should we do about cursing?
What is emotion?
How do you get a job?
What is death like? Will I see anyone I know?
Why are there Communists?
Why do people go crazy?
Why do people hate insects?

These questions are all excellent topics for study and discussion, but most of them I haven't touched upon.

Also, they asked dozens of questions you might see in "Dear Abby" or "Ask Beth," such as:

I like this boy who is my good friend's boyfriend. He likes me as a friend. I don't know, but they might be breaking up. I would want to go out with him if they break up but I'm scared I'd lose her friendship. We've been friends (good friends) for six years and I wouldn't want it to end. What should I do? —Sixth-grade girl.

Why do girls change their moods so quickly? Some girls are nice one minute and they are totally different in a second. Does this happen because they are treated in a certain way at home? If so, can I change this? I probably can't but I would like to. —Sixth-grade boy.

I haven't tried to answer such questions directly, because many of them are too individual and specific. I leave them to the excellent Abby and Beth! What I do instead is to help children find their own answers by providing (1) facts about the human body and people's feelings, (2) scientific information about how people behave in different situations, and (3) some guides for how to approach matters of love and sex as they grow older. Five are:

- Tell the truth.
- Know the facts.
- Don't harm yourself or others.
- Consider the feelings of others.
- Consider your own feelings.

Further, the girls and boys who answered the questionnaire asked a lot of *should* questions that really don't have simple, straightforward answers—such as: What age should a boy and girl be to have sex? When should I start getting sperms? Should a girl have big breasts? Should people or families keep secrets from each other?

I had to decide which questions to answer and what sort of language to use. Therefore, I set some policies for myself:

- To concentrate mainly on questions having to do with love, sex, and families—especially the first two. Otherwise the book would be too long.
- To answer only questions that were asked by several people, not just two or three.
- To use simple, standard words, even though boys' and girls' questions sometimes used slang. Why? Because slang words about sex offend and hurt some people and might make them not want to read this book. (I also corrected misspelled words and fixed up some confusing grammar.)
- To refrain from answering questions on exactly how to "do" or "make" sex. Therefore, the book tells *what is*, not *how to*. This does not mean that the book isn't honest, straightforward, and plain. I hope it is. But most (not all) of the fourth-, fifth-, and sixth-graders seemed to assume that actually "having sex" was something they would not do now but would do later. They wanted to know *now* about what would happen *later*.

Despite this restraint, however, the book does answer clearly the main questions asked.

Here are four suggestions made on four different questionnaires. I've tried to follow them as best I can.

This was quite an experience [answering the questionnaire]. *Thanks a lot. I hope that in the book you will answer the questions I asked because I want to find out about things.* —Sixth-grade girl.

I would like clear, exact diagrams, not pictures of people necking in bed. —Fourth-grade boy.

When you talk about these subjects, please don't use super-scientific names that we can't understand, but don't use slang, like "boner" instead of "erection." —Sixth-grade girl.

In each subject, make things very clear and easy to understand. Give a good end to the book. —Sixth-grade boy.

Now we start the book. But first I thank the thousand boys and girls, the dozens of teachers, and the score or so of schools that made it possible for me to know what to put in the book.

Eric W. Johnson

—1—

People—Human Beings

How did people start on earth? —*Fourth-grade boy*.

People—human beings—live on the planet Earth. Scientists believe that the earth is about 4.5 billion years old. The first life on earth was a kind of ooze that came into being around 3 to 4 billion years ago. Since then, life on earth has evolved into thousands of different kinds of creatures. Each kind is called a *species* (SPEE-sheez).* The species we now call *human beings* developed about 1.5 million years ago. However, human beings who looked just like us today developed only about 40,000 years ago. Thus, we people are rather young compared to the age of the earth and to the beginnings of life. If you represent the age of the earth as a football field 100 yards long, you could say that human beings have existed on earth for only the last ⅓ of an inch of the field.

There are some people who strongly believe in the Bible story of creation. It is told in the Book of Genesis. It says that God created the heavens and the earth and all species of life, including Adam and Eve, in six days. According to the Bible, the earth is only a few thousand years old.

How many people are there on earth? —*Sixth-grade boy*.

The number of human beings on earth used to be very small. But during the last 200 years it has been increasing fast. In 10,000

*As with *species*, the first time I use and explain a new word and show how to pronounce it, it will be printed in *italics*. Later on in the book you may forget what the word means. If you do, look it up in the index. If it's printed in the index in **boldface type**, you'll find it defined on the page numbered in **boldface**. Examples: **species, 5; prejudice, 8; uterus, 21.**

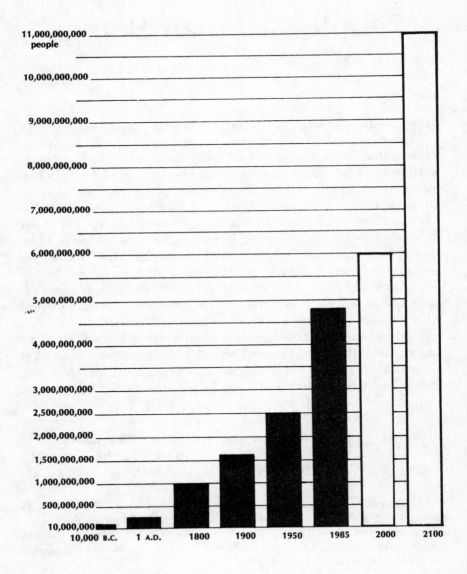

World population growth: 10,000 B.C. to 2100 A.D.

B.C., there were probably only about 10 million people on earth. By the year 1 A.D. there were about 300 million. By 1700 there were 625 million; by 1800, 910 million; by 1900, 1,600 million (1.6 billion). Today there are about 4.7 billion, and by the year 2000 there will probably be some 6 billion. Scientists guess that by about 2100 we human beings will have reached a total of about 11 billion. Sometime around then, they think, we shall stop increasing in number. However, no one is sure about these figures.

How do people reproduce themselves? *—Fifth-grade girl*.

People *reproduce*—create children—by having *sexual intercourse*, also known as "having sex." This means that a man and a woman mate, a man's sperm joins with a woman's egg, and in about nine months a baby is born. This is explained in much more detail in Chapter 2.

Who invented sex anyway? *—Fourth-grade boy*.

Sex wasn't "invented." Sexual reproduction has *evolved* (ee-VAHLVD). That is, over the years nature has changed the way animals and plants reproduce to develop the best, most efficient method for each species to create others of its kind. But there are thousands of species of life that can reproduce *non*sexually (the scientific word is *asexually*, AY-SEK-shoo-ull-ee). Some species, such as one-celled creatures like the amoeba, just divide and form two identical new creatures. Other species send out a part of themselves that develops into a new individual. For example, some plants, such as strawberries and grape vines, send out a shoot or runner. Still other species, such as mushrooms, produce spores (tiny cells), which grow into a new organism. These are all nonsexual kinds of reproduction. Among species that use them, there is no male or female.

But thousands of species do reproduce *sexually*: A sperm from the male joins with an egg from the female. A few examples of such species are dogs, cats, birds, fish, elephants, many kinds of plants, and human beings.

Of course, much of human sexual activity is not for reproduction. It is for pleasure and to express love. Also, sex can be used in bad and beautiful ways. In Chapter 4, I answer many questions about different kinds of human sexual activity.

What would happen if a person mated with a dog? —*Fifth-grade boy*.

Both people and dogs are *mammals*. Mammals are creatures that feed their young with milk from the breasts of the female. Mammals also have hair on their bodies. There are about 5,000 different species of mammals on earth. But people and dogs are two different species of mammals. When a male from one species mates with a female from a different species, no babies can be produced. When a male dog mates with a female dog, a puppy may be produced. When a man and a woman mate, a human baby may be produced. But if a person mated with a dog, nothing would be produced.

What happens when a black person and a white person have sexual intercourse? —*Sixth-grade boy*.

Blacks and whites (and all other human beings) are of one species. The most obvious difference between them is skin color. The skin of a black person has more of a pigment called *melanin* in it than the skin of a white person. Under the surface of the skin, however, they are the same. Since they are of the same species, when a black person mates with a white person, they have a human baby, and the skin color of the baby is usually somewhere between the parents' different skin colors.

Some More Questions

As I said in Chapter 1, there isn't room in this book to answer all of the many questions asked about people. However, here are some comments on a few questions that many, many boys and girls asked in one way or another and that they often seemed very worried about. My comments may help you understand better what you read in the chapters on love, sex, and families.

Why are people prejudiced? —*Fifth-grade boy*.

A *prejudice* (PREH-juh-diss) is an opinion that is formed without knowing all the facts. For example, a boy may be prejudiced against white people because he has had some bad experiences with them or heard bad things about them. So when he meets a white person, he judges that person as bad before knowing the facts about him or her as an individual. (He *pre-judges*; he is *prejudiced*.) Or a girl may be prejudiced in favor of people from a certain country because she has had good experiences with people from there—she will think that *anyone* from that country is a good person. Usually, though, when we talk about prejudice, we mean feelings *against* certain groups—for example, races, religions, nationalities, or females, males, poor people, rich people. Prejudice against groups is harmful. It's much better to find out the facts and form your opinions about each individual person on the basis of those facts.

So why are so many people prejudiced? It's because their feelings are so strong that they form their opinions too quickly. They don't look for the facts. Also, many people feel bad about themselves. They don't really respect themselves because of the way they have been treated. When people don't respect themselves, they may not respect other people, either. Sometimes they tend to try to make themselves feel better by putting other people down.

An especially cruel way of putting people down is to call them names—like sissy, retard, fag, wop, kike, nigger, or whitey. Often, people who call people names do it in fun, not to be cruel. But it's a dangerous kind of fun, and people may not show or say how much it hurts. The best policy is never to call anybody names.

Why do people laugh at other people? —*Sixth-grade girl.*

It is cruel to laugh *at* other people. It causes them to feel bad and unhappy. It's great to laugh *with* people. Life is sometimes funny. And life is sometimes difficult. To laugh about it with other people often helps to make everyone feel better.

So why do people laugh *at* others? One reason is that they don't take time to think how being laughed at will hurt the other people. If they knew, they probably wouldn't laugh. Another reason is that if you laugh at another person, it may make you *think* you're important and better than that person—the same way prejudice does. If you don't feel good about yourself, you take it out on others—by laughing at them, by being cruel.

A good rule for life is never to laugh *at* another person. Think how you feel when you are being laughed at. And if somebody laughs at you, remember, it's perfectly normal to feel bad about it. Try to find out why you are being laughed at. Maybe a friend will tell you. Or maybe you can just ask, "Why are you laughing at me? I'd like to know because it makes me feel bad." Then they'll understand how you feel and may stop. Or you may find out how you can change what you do so that you won't be laughed at. Or, if it's really funny, you can laugh too. Maybe you're a comedian!

It's especially cruel to laugh at people with handicaps. Usually, they cannot cure their handicaps. They have to live with them and manage them. One of the hardest parts of living with a handicap is being laughed at. The best thing handicapped people can do, if they are able, is to explain this and to say how much the laughter hurts. If they do this, they may help other handicapped people.

Why do people feel hatred toward each other? —*Fourth-grade girl.*

Hatred is a very strong dislike or bad feeling against a person or people. Sometimes people hate others who do bad things to them. Or they may hate others because they've heard bad things about them. Still another reason for hating someone is that he or she has something you want and won't share it or give it to you, and you feel that is unfair.

It is quite natural to feel hatred toward other people at times. It is also part of human nature to explain hard times or failure by picking out an enemy. Sometimes you feel hatred toward someone you know very well and live very close to. Often, this is because they do something you don't like, or they put you down, get in your way, or prevent you from doing or getting what you want. Usually, such feelings of hate don't last long. They pass. It's important to remember this. Even most people who really love each other feel hate toward each other now and then. In Chapter 3, when I talk about love, I'll say more about this. When a feeling of hate comes over you, it is very important not to do something that will make it worse—such as hitting or saying very cruel things. Instead, *think* about it.

Why do people have feelings? What do you do about them? Are they bad? —*Sixth-grade girl*.

Of course, we all have feelings. One feeling is hate, which we've just talked about. It feels bad to hate. Another feeling is love. It feels good to love. Other feelings are jealousy, anger, sadness, joy, boredom, cheerfulness. Why do we have feelings? It's because we are human beings who have minds and emotions. When we see and hear things and people, we naturally react to them.

It is important to remember that people cannot always control their feelings. If you suddenly feel, "I hate Marge for doing that," or "I love Kim whenever he talks that way," or "I feel mad at so-and-so!" those are feelings, and they're difficult to control. They just come over you. However, you *are* responsible for what you *do* about your feelings—how you act. You usually can control your actions. You certainly should try to. You may feel mad at somebody and want to hit him or her, maybe even your brother or mother or classmate or friend. You can't help that feeling. But you can control your actions. Therefore, you don't hit your mother. You just feel mad.

So are feelings bad? No. We just have them. But if we have a lot of feelings that may make us want to do harmful things, it's very helpful to talk with somebody about them. Talk with your mother or father, a grandparent, a friend, a teacher—someone you can trust and be calm with.

What happens when people lose their temper? —*Fifth-grade boy*.

Most people are in control of themselves most of the time. They live and work and play with other people without losing their temper. They may feel angry from time to time, but they don't lose control. However, sometimes they may feel tired. Or maybe things have gone badly for them, or people have treated them meanly. Then they get so angry, so mad, that they lose their temper. Then they shout or scream or hit, or slam doors, or say very angry things, or call other people names.

It's just something that most human beings do now and then. After they lose their temper, sometimes they feel better, especially if they just go off and get angry all by themselves. Maybe they kick a tree or pound a wall or run around the block. They get it out of their system. But other times, they lose their temper by doing and saying things that make other people feel bad, or they may actually hit them and hurt them.

So what can you do if you have lost your temper? You can apologize; just say, "I'm sorry!" Later, you can explain why you lost your temper so others will understand. Also, you can learn to notice the signs that you are about to lose your temper and say to yourself, "Watch it!" That often helps you not to lose control.

If someone loses his or her temper at you, try to stay calm. Also, you can try not to hold a grudge. If someone says something very mean to you, remember that the person has lost control over his or her temper. You can do the same even if you get hit. You can try to keep calm. And then, when the anger has passed, try to talk about it. If it's someone you love, you might try to find a way to say, "I love you"—even if you didn't love the anger and loss of temper.

Is it bad for people to lose their tempers? If they do it a lot, yes, it is bad. But most of us lose our tempers from time to time, and it doesn't mean the end of the world.

Why do people hit each other? —*Fourth-grade girl.*
   A great many boys and girls asked this question. Most people hit each other because they get angry and lose their temper. When people live together or work closely together (as in school), they sometimes want the same things. Or they get in each other's way. Or one will seem to have insulted the other. And the first thing they know, they've hit each other.

Sometimes they just don't know what else to do, and so they hit. Quite often they feel very sorry afterward. Therefore, it's important not to believe that just because you hit someone, you're going to hate him or her forever, or the other way around if it was you who got hit.

Another reason people hit others is that they feel angry about things that have nothing to do with the person they hit. Maybe a boy has been given a tough time by his parents, for example, and he needs to get rid of his anger. So he "takes it out" on a brother or sister. Parents may take out their anger on their children too.

If you find you're doing a lot of hitting, think about it. Try to figure out why. When you're calm, talk with someone about it—maybe even the person you've been hitting—and figure it out together. Try to do the same thing if you're the one who's getting hit. Hitting is almost always a bad thing to do. It hurts people, both their bodies and their feelings. Also, it rarely solves any problems.

Why do people abuse children? —*Fifth-grade boy.*

We've just talked about why people lose their temper and hit each other. When people believe that life is very hard on them—for instance, if they can't get a job, or have trouble at work, or have too much to do around the house—they tend to feel angry. When they can't manage things very well, and when they feel hateful, they tend to hit out at others. Since children are smaller than parents, it's often the children who get hit. When the hitting is really bad, it's called *child abuse.*

Another kind of child abuse is with words—frequent shouting, teasing, and cruel laughter. This kind of abuse can be just as harmful as hitting.

One reason for abuse is that quite often children really need things that their parents can't give them. Or they need time to talk and be loved, and their parents can't seem to give that time because life is so hard. So the children cry and complain and seem to get in the way. This makes the parents—or a parent—angry, even though *it's not the child's fault.* The child's needs are important. Another kind of child abuse has to do with sex. In Chapter 4, pages 82–83, I will discuss that problem.

If children are being abused, they need help, and they should try to find someone to talk to and get help. Sometimes grand-parents can help. So can teachers or advisers at school. An understanding neighbor or the parent of a friend could also be approached. Of course, the parents who are doing the abusing need help too.

Why do parents sometimes beat the kid and not the problem? —*Fifth-grade girl.*

A good question. I suppose it's because they get angry, and when people are angry, they don't think clearly. What to do about it? If you can, say something like "I don't understand why you're so angry. It frightens me." Then listen to the answer you get. Maybe the talking and listening will reduce the anger. Then you and your parents can start beating the problem.

I don't think parents should hit children. It just makes me more of a bad child. They don't abuse me, but they give a slap or two—or three, or four. I like to use a dog as an example. Dogs turn wild and mad when their masters hit them a lot.   —*Sixth-grade girl.*

It's true. Dogs turn wild and mad, or they act afraid and slink around unhappily. Children are different from dogs, of course, but they can turn wild, and they can get scared and timid. That's not good.

The answer: Again, try to find times to talk and to listen.

Why do people tell lies to each other?   —*Fourth-grade girl.*

Many boys and girls asked this question in one way or another. The answer is very complicated, and there are lots of answers. One is that people tell lies because they are afraid that the truth will get them into trouble. For example, if a girl stole something, she may lie and say she didn't. If a boy damaged something in the house, he may lie and say he didn't. If girls and boys don't do their homework, they may make up a false excuse to explain why.

Or people may lie and claim to have read schoolbooks they haven't, or to have friends they don't, or to be champions at something they're not—all because they want other people to think well of them. Or they may make up a lie just for the fun of it.

All the lies I just mentioned are bad lies. But sometimes people tell what they think are good lies. For example, they don't want to hurt a person's feelings. Suppose a woman asks you, "How do you like my new hairdo?" or a man asks, "What do you think of my new suit?" Even if you don't like the hairdo or the suit, you'll probably say, "Very nice" or "Really fashionable!" instead of "Not much" or "It looks terrible." Thoughtful people may find ways to tell the truth gently—or at least not to tell an actual lie—saying something like, "It's really interesting."

But a more serious reason why some people tell lies is that

they think the truth may be really harmful for someone else. This probably explains why some parents don't tell their children the truth about sex. They're afraid the information will be harmful to the children. But it's much better to tell the truth about sex, or else to say, truthfully, "I think you're too young to know about that, but I'll tell you when you are older." There's more about this in Chapter 4, pages 69–71. Also, in Chapter 5, pp. 106–114, I discuss the questions boys and girls ask about why parents often don't tell the truth about their own marriages, divorces, and feelings toward each other.

Why are some people better-looking than others? —*Sixth-grade boy*.

Quite a few boys and girls asked about this. Most of them believed that others were better-looking than they themselves were. This really troubled them. Obviously, there's no single answer to the question. People are born so that they will grow up to look different from other people. Some will be tall, some short; their eyes will be blue or brown or another color; the shapes of their noses, mouths, and ears will be different. All these features are *inherited*. They come from each person's father and mother, and grandparents, and ancestors even further back. One just has to accept the looks that one is born with.

Fortunately, however, people have different tastes about what "good-looking" means. So people like and fall in love with people of all appearances, shapes, and sizes. You don't have to worry about whether you look like what you think is the best-looking boy or girl in the class, or on TV, or in a magazine. There are lots of ways to look good.

Furthermore, what you do with yourself helps to make you attractive—or unattractive. The clothes you wear, how you stand and sit, your weight, the expression on your face, the way you respond to other people, even the way you feel about yourself, all affect the way other people see you. And all these things are things you *can* change.

However, just look around and see how many different kinds of people are attracted to each other. Often, simple looks have little to do with it. It has more to do with personality. And your personality is something you can work on.

Why are some people bigger than others? Is it good to be larger? —*Sixth-grade boy.*

Many boys and girls worry about this. Just like looks, your size depends mostly on what you inherit from your parents. Some people are born to be tall, some to be short, some to be medium-size. Others are born to be heavy or thin or average in weight. Some have to work hard to lose weight; others have a hard time gaining it. There are people of all sizes and shapes who are happy and unhappy, popular and unpopular. So no one can say whether it's "good" to be larger.

Another thing that boys and girls worry about is whether they are "the right size for my age." The fact is that young people develop at different rates. Some are bigger than most of their classmates in fifth grade, yet by the time they are in high school, others have "caught up" and are just as big. Some, on the other hand, are very small in early grades and suddenly grow a lot later on. (I say more about this in Chapter 2.)

Is it OK to date a boy smaller than you? —*Fifth-grade girl.*

Of course it is. Size has very little to do with whom you should date. Other questions, asked by many, are about when to start dating and what to do on dates. I discuss those questions in later chapters.

Why are some people more popular than others? —*Fifth-grade girl.*

Most boys and girls certainly do worry about this problem. There is no magic formula for being "popular." Some people are popular because they are very pleasant to other people; some because they are interesting talkers; some because they listen well; some because they are very good-looking; some because they are good athletes; some because they have money; some because they are funny and make people laugh; some because they are comfortable and easy to be with. Also, some people don't want to be popular—they'd rather just have a few good friends. And popularity comes and goes. Some people are well liked in fourth grade, but by eight grade they have a hard time getting along with others—and then by eleventh grade they have lots of friends again.

If you are very worried about not being popular or having friends, talk to someone about it, someone you can trust even if you don't really know them very well. They may be able to help you see yourself the way other people see you. And that may help you make friends with people. Maybe you're doing things that other people don't like. If you really want to, you can probably change those things.

Talking with a person you trust would also be useful to answer the next question.

Why do I feel so "out" of my group? —*Sixth-grade boy*.

Lots of people feel that way, and it's a hard feeling to have. One thing that can help people make friends is developing a skill in some area—music, sports, acting, or carpentry, for instance. A well-developed skill gives a person confidence and also provides a way to get to know other people with the same interests.

Which are smarter, boys or girls? —*Fourth-grade boy*.

A famous writer of dictionaries, Dr. Samuel Johnson (1709–1794), was once asked, "Which are more intelligent, women or men?" He replied with a question: "*Which* woman? *Which* man?" There's your answer! Boys and girls, men and women, are much more alike than different. They are both members of the same species, human beings. Some are more intelligent than others, but no one can truthfully say that one sex is more intelligent than the other.

One of the things that make people interesting is that they have many different *kinds* of intelligence. Some are very smart with words, others at making rules, others at understanding how people feel, still others at making decisions.

Certainly, there's a lot more to intelligence than what is measured by so-called "intelligence tests" or grades in school, even though these are important.

What should you do if you are offered drugs, alcohol, or cigarettes? *—Sixth-grade boy.*

The answer is plain and simple: Turn them down. Drugs (except for those used to cure sickness), alcohol, and tobacco are bad for your health. It is risky for young people to use them. For some boys and girls, it is a great temptation to try them. They've heard about the pleasures they bring. They may feel "out of it" or immature if they don't try what the really "in" people are using. Well, it doesn't make sense, no matter what arguments people use on you. It's mature and sensible to stay healthy; it's immature and foolish to risk hurting your health.

"Yes, but it's really *not* that simple," some readers will say. On their questionnaires, many boys and girls wrote about pressure from friends and classmates—*peer pressure*, it's called. They asked: **What do you do if you have to smoke to be cool?** *—Fifth-grade girl.*

My friend uses drugs, and she asks me, 'What's the matter? Just try it. It's cool.' What do I do about that? *—Sixth-grade girl.*

I agree that it's often not simple to refuse to do what you think "everybody" is doing. Peer pressure is tough to resist, especially when you want to be popular with those who are popular. And it gets even tougher when you're a teenager. However, work up your courage, use your brains, and start a little peer pressure of your own! Remember, *everybody* isn't doing it. And you don't win real, healthy respect from others because you smoke or use drugs. So I repeat: It's immature and foolish to risk hurting your health.

I'll end this chapter on people with the words a fifth-grade girl wrote on her questionnaire: "People are all different in color, shape, size, and age. I think it doesn't matter what color, shape, size or age you are. . . . Some adults think kids are not people, but we kids *are* people, just like adults"—and, I can add, just as different from each other as adults are.

—2—

How Human Beings
Reproduce

The questions most frequently asked, in many different ways, by fourth-, fifth-, and sixth-graders were: **How do people have babies? Exactly what happens? How do men's bodies and women's bodies work to have children?** These are questions about the *reproductive system*. And many boys and girls went on to say, "Use clear diagrams"; "Show us pictures."

The second most frequently asked questions had to do with feelings: **What does having sex feel like? Does it feel good? Does sex hurt? Is sex dirty? Is sex the best thing in the world?**

First, I'll explain how people have babies, how they *reproduce*. Later, in Chapter 4, I'll talk about sex and feelings. As you read these chapters, you will learn that sex for reproduction—to have babies—is one part of sex. Sex for good feelings and pleasure is another part of sex. They are not the same, but they are closely related.

Now here are the facts about reproduction—first about women, then about men.

The woman's reproductive system

As you read this explanation, look at the illustration and labels on the next page. We'll start at the upper end of the woman's reproductive system.

Inside a woman's body are two organs called *ovaries* (OH-va-reez). There is one ovary on each side of her abdomen, or belly. Each ovary contains thousands of tiny unripe eggs, which are

19

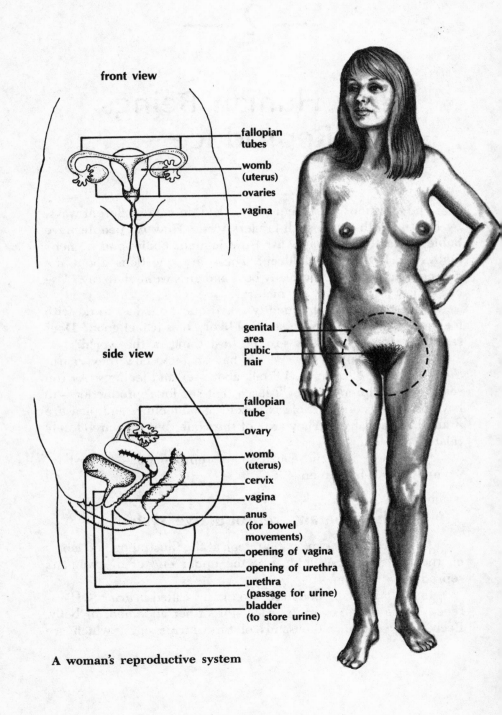

front view

fallopian tubes

womb (uterus)

ovaries

vagina

genital area

pubic hair

side view

fallopian tube

ovary

womb (uterus)

cervix

vagina

anus (for bowel movements)

opening of vagina

opening of urethra

urethra (passage for urine)

bladder (to store urine)

A woman's reproductive system

called *ova* (OH-vuh). Once a month, more or less, an egg (*ovum*) ripens and bursts from one of the two ovaries. This process is called *ovulation* (AH-vyoo-LAY-shun). The egg enters one of the two *fallopian* (fa-LO-pee-un) *tubes*, and it is slowly moved down that tube until it reaches the woman's *uterus* (YEW-tuh-russ)—also called her *womb* (woom).

When a woman has sexual intercourse with a man, his *sperms* travel through the uterus and up the fallopian tubes. If intercourse takes place around the time a woman ovulates, the egg meets the sperms in the fallopian tube before it gets to the uterus. One sperm enters the egg and *fertilizes* (FUR-ti-ly-zez) it. This is called *conception* (kun-SEP-shun). A new life is *conceived*, has started to develop. This fertilized egg is moved on down the tube. As it travels, it has already begun to grow. It is now called an *embryo* (EM-bree-oh). The embryo implants itself in the thick, soft lining of the uterus, which provides a comfortable place for its development. There it will grow for about 266 days (nine months) until it is ready to be born as a baby. (The growth and birth of the baby are explained in detail later in this chapter.)

The uterus is an amazing organ. When a woman is not pregnant, it is only about three inches long. But it can stretch enough to hold a baby until it is ready to be born. The uterus walls contain very powerful muscles, which push the baby out at birth.

Often, people say that the baby grows in its mother's stomach. This is not so. It grows in that special place, the uterus, which is quite far below the stomach and entirely separate from it.

We started this explanation of the woman's reproductive system at the ovary end. Now let's describe it from the lower end. At this end are the woman's *genitals* (JEN-i-tuls). Look at the illustration on page 22. The genitals are the external parts of the reproductive system, located on the *outside* of the body, unlike the uterus. A woman's genitals include the opening to her *vagina* (va-JY-nuh) and *labia* (LAY-bee-uh), the fleshy lips that cover it. They are located between her legs toward the front. This area is called the *vulva* (VULL-vuh). Another part of the vulva is the *clitoris* (CLIT-er-iss), but the clitoris is not a reproductive organ. It is a sexual-feeling organ, and it is discussed in Chapter 4.

Look at the illustration on page 20. As you see there, the vagina is just behind the *urethra* (yew-REE-thruh), the passage for urine. Even farther back is the woman's *anus* (AY-nus), the opening for her bowel movements.

The *vagina* is a soft passageway about three to four inches long. This is where a man puts his penis during sexual intercourse. At the upper end of the vagina is the *cervix* (SUR-vix). The cervix is the opening to the uterus.

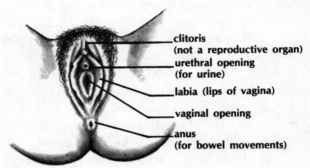

clitoris
(not a reproductive organ)
urethral opening
(for urine)
labia (lips of vagina)
vaginal opening
anus
(for bowel movements)

Female genital area

The cervix and the vagina together are often referred to as the *birth canal*, since this is the passageway through which the baby will come out after its nine months of growing in the uterus. The vagina, like the uterus, is a very elastic organ; it must be able to stretch wide enough for the baby's journey out of the uterus during birth.

Menstruation

If a woman does not have sexual intercourse around the time she ovulates, or if she uses a method of *birth control* (see Chapter 4), the egg will not be fertilized. This means that the soft, thick lining inside the uterus—the *endometrium* (en-doh-MEE-tree-um)—will not be needed, so about once a month the uterus sheds this lining. This process is called *menstruation* (MEN-stroo-AY-shun). When a woman menstruates, she is "having her period."

The monthly flow of menstruation lasts from three to seven days; it's different from one woman to the next. The flow contains blood and tissue. But it is not like ordinary bleeding. The woman's body is just getting rid of extra blood and tissue that are no longer needed.

Growing up

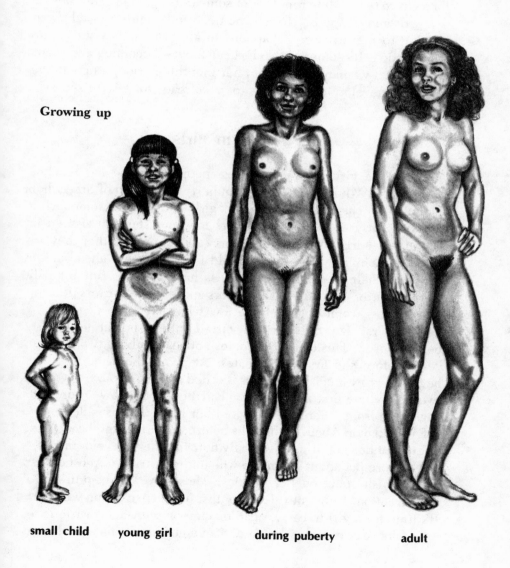

small child   **young girl**   **during puberty**   **adult**

When a woman menstruates, she wears a *pad* in her panties to absorb the flow. Or she may put a *tampon*, also made of absorbent material, in her vagina. She should change the pads or tampons quite often, throwing the old ones away. Pads and tampons come with written instructions that should be read carefully. It is helpful for a girl to talk with her mother or some other person about how to use pads and tampons. There is no need to be embarrassed about starting to menstruate. It happens to all girls as they grow into womanhood. It's something to be glad about—becoming a woman.

Once a woman has finished her monthly period, a new lining begins to develop in her uterus to make ready for a fertilized egg.

Puberty in girls

When a girl first menstruates, people say she has reached *puberty* (PEW-bur-tee). Actually, puberty is a period of time when a lot of other changes take place in a girl's body too. In some girls it starts as early as age eight. Others may not start till sixteen or seventeen. Girls (and boys, too) worry a lot about whether they are ahead or behind "where they should be." Are they "ahead of" or "behind" their friends? The worry is hard to take. But it really doesn't matter. Both the early starters and the late starters develop into mature women. About the few who don't, see page 39.

The first sign that a girl has started puberty is that her breasts begin to grow. This usually becomes noticeable about two or three years before she first menstruates. At about the same age, she begins to grow much faster. This is called a *growth spurt*. A year or two before she first menstruates, hair begins to grow around her vagina, in front where her legs join her body. This is called *pubic* (PEW-bik) hair. About six months before menstruation, hair begins to grow under her arms as well. By noticing these developments, a girl can predict about when she will first menstruate. Another sign is yellowish spots on her panties. These are the beginnings of menstruation. In the next few months, full menstruation will start. It's time for a girl to carry a pad or tampon with her, just in case.

A lot of boys and girls asked, **Can a girl have a baby if she has** sex before she has her first period? The answer is: *Yes*, it happens. Some girls can and do. That is, some girls ovulate before they first menstruate. Most girls, though, can't become pregnant until a few months after they first menstruate.

Another part of a woman's reproductive system is her *breasts*. When a woman has a baby, her breasts swell. Inside the breasts are glands that make milk. The baby sucks the milk from its mother's *nipples*.

The man's reproductive system

As you read this section, look at the illustrations and labels on the next page.

A man's reproductive organs, his *genitals* (JEN-i-tuls) are mostly outside his body. His most obvious organ is his *penis* (PEE-nuss). It is usually about the length of a finger but larger around. Penises differ greatly in size. This difference is not important (unless a person *thinks* it is). Big penises and little penises work equally well as reproductive organs.

uncircumcised

circumcised

When a boy is born, the end of his penis is covered by *foreskin*. This skin can be pushed back. Often the doctor cuts off the foreskin soon after a baby boy is born. This operation is called *circumcision* (SUR-kum-SIZH-un). Some religions require circumcision, and some doctors and parents believe it makes it easier to keep the end of the penis clean. Both circumcised and uncircumcised penises work equally well as far as reproduction and sexual pleasure are concerned.

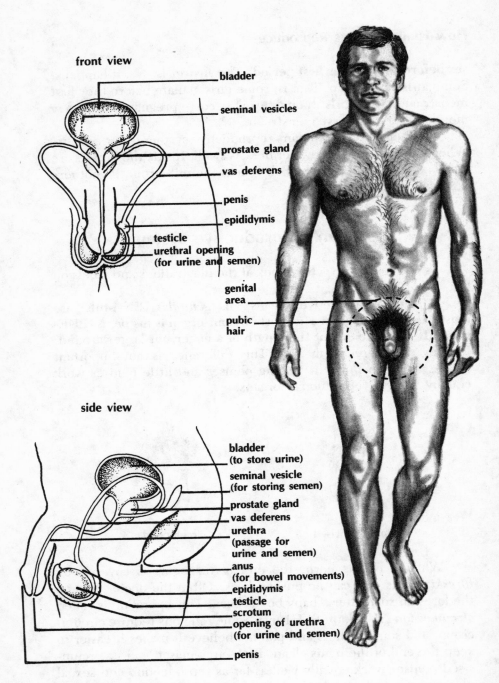

front view

bladder

seminal vesicles

prostate gland

vas deferens

penis

epididymis

testicle
urethral opening
(for urine and semen)

genital
area

pubic
hair

side view

bladder
(to store urine)

seminal vesicle
(for storing semen)

prostate gland
vas deferens
urethra
(passage for
urine and semen)

anus
(for bowel movements)

epididymis
testicle
scrotum
opening of urethra
(for urine and semen)

penis

A man's reproductive system

Under the penis hangs a loose, wrinkly sac of skin called the *scrotum* (SKROH-tum). Inside the scrotum are two organs called *testicles* (TESS-ti-kulz) or *testes* (TESS-teez). They are oval-shaped, and in a grown man each one is about 1 1/2 inches long. Often one is slightly larger than the other and hangs a bit lower. The testicles make sperms, millions and millions of them; they look like tiny tadpoles but are so small that you can see them only through a microscope. The sperms pass from each testicle through about half a mile of tiny coiled-up tubes called the *epididymis* (eh-puh-DI-di-muss). As they travel along, the sperms are growing and maturing. Then they enter two larger tubes called the *vas deferens* (VASS DEF-uh-renz). The sperms are stored in the vas and in two little sacs called *seminal vesicles* (SEM-in-al VES-i-kulz). The seminal vesicles are located behind the man's *prostate* (PRAH-stayt) *gland*. The prostate gland makes a thick, whitish liquid that mixes with the sperms. This mixture is called *semen* (SEE-min). It is milky-looking and has a very particular smell.

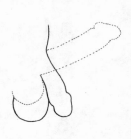

When a man is sexually excited, and at certain other times (for example, when he first wakes up and needs to urinate), his penis becomes much thicker, longer, and harder. It stands out stiffly from his body at an angle. This is called an *erection* (ee-REK-shun). If a man reaches a peak of sexual excitement, semen (containing sperms) will spurt out of his penis. This is called an *ejaculation* (ee-JAK-yoo-LAY-shun). The man ejaculates the sperms through a tube in his penis called the *urethra* (yew-REE-thruh). It is the same passage through which urine flows from his bladder when he urinates. However, a man cannot urinate and ejaculate at the same time. A special valve inside his body automatically shuts off the urine when his penis is erect and he is going to ejaculate.

During intercourse, the semen is ejaculated into the woman's vagina. You have already read about how sperm meets egg and fertilizes it. A later section of this chapter tells more about that and what happens afterward.

Most men have a number of erections during the day and night. Almost all of them end without any semen being ejaculated.

Growing up

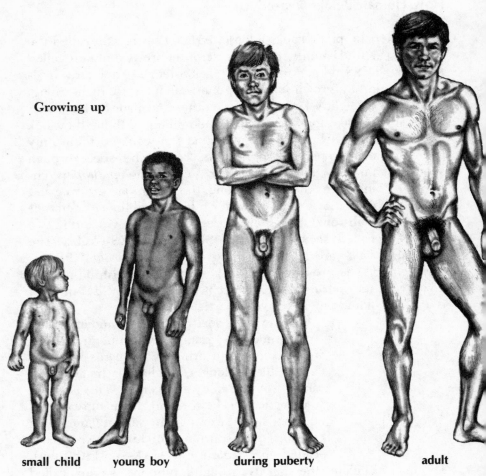

small child   young boy   during puberty   adult

Puberty in boys

When a boy first ejaculates semen, people say he has reached *puberty* (PEW-bur-tee). Puberty is a period of time when many changes take place in a boy's body. It may start anywhere from around age nine to seventeen. The average age for first ejaculation of semen is about thirteen, but it's perfectly normal for it to happen earlier or later than that. (Note that from birth on, or even before birth, boys' penises become erect, but they do not ejaculate semen until puberty.) The first sign that puberty is coming is the start of a quick *growth spurt* of the body. It usually begins a year or two later in boys than in girls. There's a period of time when many girls are larger than most of their male classmates. The surest sign that a boy will soon ejaculate is the appearance of curly hair above his penis—*pubic* (PEW-bik) hair. A boy's *change of voice* usually comes a few months *after* he reaches puberty.

Many boys worry about whether they are "ahead of" or "behind" other boys they know. Are they developing too fast or too slowly? It's easy to understand why boys worry about this. However, it's a useless worry. Almost all boys will mature into men—some sooner, some later. (About that "almost," see page 39.)

Sexual intercourse and fertilization

As you already know, it is by sexual intercourse that human beings reproduce. Women's bodies contain eggs. Men's bodies make sperms. To conceive a baby, a man puts his erect penis into a woman's vagina. After a time of sexually stimulating movements, the penis ejaculates semen into the vagina. (Some semen may also "leak" out before a man ejaculates, so conception *can* take place without ejaculation.) The average ejaculation, about a teaspoonful of semen, contains about 150 million to 600 million sperms. That's a vast number! One could say that it's nature's way of making sure there are enough sperms so that some of them will make it all the way to the egg. Most of them die or get lost on the way and then are simply and harmlessly absorbed by the woman's body.

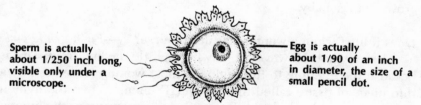

Sperm is actually about 1/250 inch long, visible only under a microscope.

Egg is actually about 1/90 of an inch in diameter, the size of a small pencil dot.

Size of egg and sperm cells compared

Some of the semen travels through the cervix and into the uterus. From there, some of the sperms make their way into the fallopian tubes. If the woman has ovulated, the sperms that have

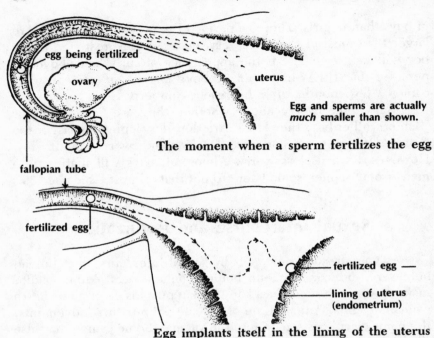

egg being fertilized

ovary

uterus

Egg and sperms are actually *much* smaller than shown.

The moment when a sperm fertilizes the egg

fallopian tube

fertilized egg

fertilized egg —

lining of uterus (endometrium)

Egg implants itself in the lining of the uterus

made it this far—probably about 2,000 of them—gather around the egg, which is traveling down one of the tubes. One sperm—only one—breaks through the outside of the egg and *fertilizes* (FUR-ti-ly-zez) it. A new cell is formed, made up of the egg and the sperm. That cell is called a *zygote* (ZY-goat). The zygote, which is already growing, moves down the fallopian tube. In two or three days, it implants itself in the soft lining of the woman's uterus. There, it grows into a baby.

Does it hurt when a woman has intercourse? —*Fifth-grade girl*.

Usually not. However, it may hurt a little the first time. This is because the opening to the vagina in most women is covered by a thin piece of tissue called the *hymen* (HY-men). When the hymen breaks, it may bleed a little. However, in many women, the hymen has already been stretched to leave a large enough opening. Also, if a woman has used tampons, that will have stretched the hymen.

In Chapter 4, I answer more questions about sexual intercourse—what men and women do, and how it feels.

How the baby grows inside the mother's uterus

When the fertilized egg (the zygote) implants itself in the lining of the uterus, it continues to grow. The woman is now pregnant. About nine months later, if all goes well, she will give

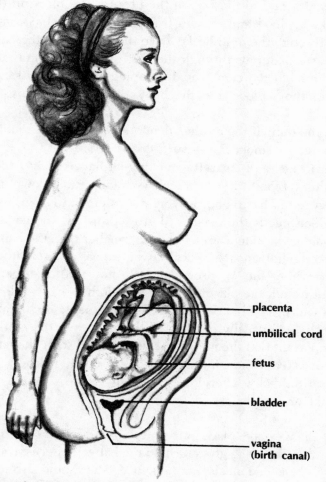

placenta

umbilical cord

fetus

bladder

vagina
(birth canal)

A mother in her ninth month of pregnancy

birth to a live baby. During the first three months after fertilization, the new life is called an embryo. From then until birth, it is called a *fetus* (FEE-tuss). (See illustration on page 31.)

The developing baby in the uterus needs nourishment and oxygen. It gets these through a cord called the *umbilical* (um-BILL-i-cul) *cord*. This cord goes from the baby's abdomen to the *placenta* (pla-SEN-tuh). The placenta is a spongy collection of tiny blood vessels attached to the wall of the uterus. The blood in the placenta picks up food and oxygen from the mother's blood and passes them through the umbilical cord to the baby. Also, the baby gets rid of waste materials through the cord, to the placenta, and into the mother's bloodstream. The developing baby makes its own blood. The mother's blood and the baby's blood do not mix.

Does it hurt the baby if the mother drinks alcohol? What about if she takes drugs or smokes? —*Sixth-grade girl.*

Alcohol, drugs, and cigarette-smoking all have strong effects on the mother's blood. For instance, smoking cuts down the amount of oxygen in her blood, leaving not as much to share with the fetus, which needs the oxygen to grow properly. In fact, the babies of women who smoke are often born smaller than the babies of women who do not smoke. Basically, whatever is in the mother's bloodstream while she is pregnant will get into the baby's bloodstream through the placenta. So if the mother drinks a lot of alcohol, this will probably harm the developing baby. If she takes drugs, the baby will usually be affected the same way the mother is. So it is important that the mother be very careful what she takes into her body. Heavy smoking or drinking, or using drugs, are likely to harm the baby. Therefore, pregnant mothers should not smoke, drink, or use drugs.

A lot of changes take place in the mother's body from the time she gets pregnant until she gives birth to the baby. It's necessary for her to eat well-balanced meals, not junk food. She should also see a doctor regularly to be sure everything is going well.

How can a woman know if she's pregnant? Is there any test?
—*Fifth-grade girl.*

Usually, the first sign of pregnancy is that the woman misses her menstrual period. (However, some women miss a period now and then for other reasons.) Another sign in many women is that their breasts grow larger and feel tender. Also, in the early months of pregnancy, some women feel sick at the stomach, or they don't feel like eating, or they may feel quite tired a lot of the time.

If a woman has been having sexual intercourse and notices any of these signs, she should check to see if she really is pregnant. A doctor or clinic can find out by testing her blood or urine. She can also buy a pregnancy testing kit at the drugstore. These kits are not always reliable, but they're better than nothing.

What decides whether you're going to get a boy or girl baby?
—*Fourth-grade boy.*

The sperm cell from the man determines this. If the sperm that enters the egg carries a *Y* chromosome, the baby will develop into a boy. If the sperm carries an *X* chromosome (KROH-muh-soam), it will be a girl. It's a matter of chance. Once the sperm has entered the egg, the question of the baby's sex is decided. Nothing can change that decision.

How do twins happen? —*Fifth-grade boy.*

There are two ways twins start. One way is when a single fertilized egg divides into two separate zygotes. Then each one develops separately into a baby. Since there was only one sperm involved, both babies will be the same sex—two boys or two girls. Also, since they both come from the same egg and sperm, they will look very much like each other. It will be hard to tell them apart. They are called *identical twins*.

The other way twins start is when two eggs are released from the ova at about the same time and fertilized by different sperms. Each fertilized egg will grow to be a baby. They will look no more alike than ordinary brothers and sisters do. They may be both boys, both girls, or one boy and one girl. They are called *fraternal twins*.

Triplets, quadruplets, and quintuplets, (three, four, or five babies born at the same time) can happen by either of those two methods as well (by one fertilized egg dividing or by separate eggs being fertilized), or by both methods happening at once. They are very rare.

Now, lets get back to the growth of the baby in the mother's uterus. Remember, when it all starts—at the moment of conception—the fertilized cell is unbelievably tiny. The egg is about the size of the period at the end of this sentence. The sperm so small you can see it only with a miscroscope. After a month of growing, the embryo is about 1/4 inch long. At the end of two months, it's about 1 inch long, still hardly noticeable. By five months, it has grown to be 10 inches long, and it weighs about 3/4 of a pound. After about nine months, it has grown to weigh about 7 or 8 pounds and is ready to be born. It has developed from a single cell to 200 billion cells! (See the pictures below. They show the real size of an embryo at eight weeks and of a fetus at thirteen and seventeen weeks.)

Three Stages of embryo and fetus, shown actual size

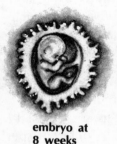

embryo at 8 weeks

fetus at 13 weeks

The embryo (and then fetus) grows inside the mother's uterus in a sac filled with a liquid called *amniotic* (AM-nee-OTT-ick) *fluid*. This fluid helps protect the baby from being bumped or harmed.

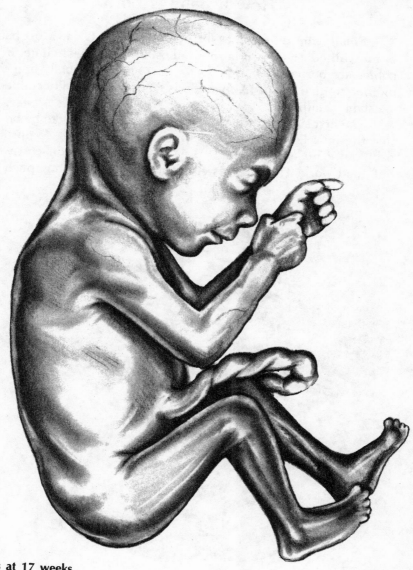

fetus at 17 weeks

How a baby is born

Finally, the time comes for the baby to be born. Most babies in the United States are born in a hospital or special clinic. Some babies are born at home. A doctor or a *midwife* usually helps the mother to give birth. (A midwife is someone specially trained to assist in childbirth.)

The first sign that the time has come for the baby to be born is that the muscles of the mother's uterus start working to push the baby out. This is called *labor* (LAY-burr)—and it is difficult work, but good work! The muscles contract very hard as they push and

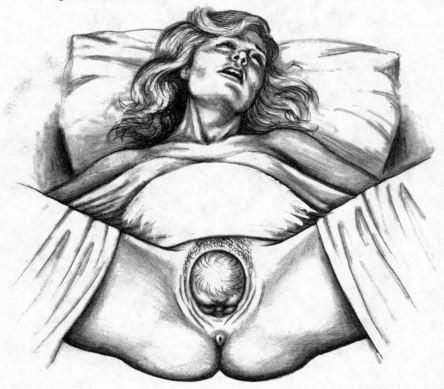

push. The labor can be quite painful. The mother may stay in labor anywhere from just a few minutes to a whole day or longer. Before the baby is born, the sac surrounding it breaks, and the amniotic fluid pours out. This is called "the rush of waters." Very soon after that the baby follows.

Soon after the baby is born, the umbilical cord is cut. This is painless. Then, very soon, the uterus pushes out the *afterbirth*, which is made up of the placenta and the remains of the sac the baby grew in. The afterbirth is thrown away. (The small circular place in the middle of your abdomen—your belly button, or *navel* (NAY-vul)—is where your umbilical cord was attached to you.)

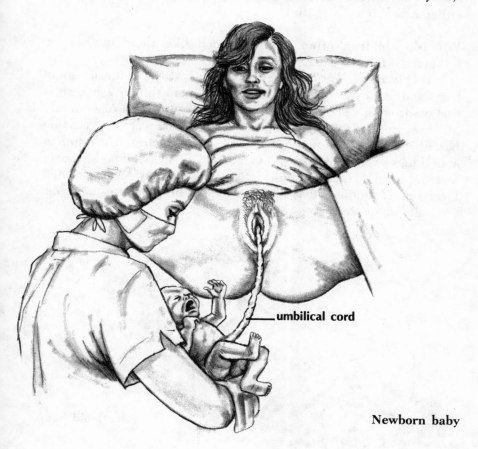

umbilical cord

Newborn baby

What newborn babies are like

At first, most newborn babies look very tired, splotchy, and wrinkled. They've just been through quite an experience! They have to get used to living in air and breathing, not living in fluid. They cry quite a lot, which is a way for them to say, "I need something." Usually, what they need is to be held and cuddled, and also to suck. They love to suck and will suck on anything. They usually get their food—milk—from their mother's breasts, sucking it from the nipples. They can also get it from a bottle with a nipple on it. They love to be held and cuddled while they nurse, from either a breast or a bottle.

Why do children often look so much like their mother or father? —*Fourth-grade boy.*

It's because of *heredity* (heh-RED-i-tee). We all inherit a lot of traits and features from our parents. The main thing we inherit is that we are human beings, not mice or elephants or walruses or any other creatures. But often we also inherit a lot of features from one parent—or perhaps a mixture of both. These include such noticeable things as color of eyes and hair and skin, shape of body, size of feet and hands. However, nobody is exactly like his or her parents. Everyone is unique—that is, there's only one person exactly like you, and that's you.

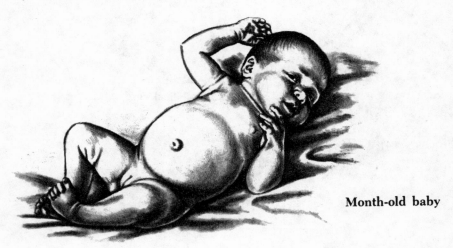

Month-old baby

All those inherited features are passed down from our parents in the egg and sperm that joined to start us off. Each egg and sperm contains *genes* (jeens), and each egg and sperm contains thousands and thousands of them. (The study of genes is called *genetics*, je-NET-icks.)

But how we develop in life depends on more than just heredity (what we get from the mixing of the genes of our parents). The other major influence is our *environment*, the kind of life that surrounds us—people, things, events, food, education, where we live, and so forth.

Thus, each person in the world is a product of his or her genes and environment.

Aren't there some people who don't develop normally? What should they do? —*Sixth-grade girl*.

Yes, a small proportion of people do not develop normally, physically and sexually. Earlier in the book, I emphasized that great differences in the age and rate of development *are* normal. Therefore, most people don't need to worry about whether they're "ahead of" or "behind" others their age. To remind yourself of this, look again at the illustrations.

However, it's true that a few boys and girls do not mature normally. They have special medical problems that require the attention of a doctor. Such help is available. Young people who are seriously concerned about their development should talk with their parents. They probably should go to their own doctor, or to a doctor or specialist at a clinic. I repeat: Help is available. People with development problems can be helped.

All right, I think I've answered the main questions boys and girls asked about how people reproduce. Now we turn to an even more complicated subject, love. It's possible to be pretty factual and scientific about reproduction. It's impossible to be so factual and scientific about love.

—3—

Love—What Is It? What Do We Do and Feel About It?

I said that it's hard to be scientific about love. Here are a few of the many questions from boys and girls that show how complicated the subject is:

What is love? How does it work? What does it do? What makes it? Does it do something to the mind? —*Fourth-grade boy.*

What is love made from? How does love happen? Is love hard to keep? Is love sweet, or is it a terrible thing to find? —*Fifth-grade girl.*

Is love funny sometimes? Is love nice in a way? —*Fifth-grade girl.*

What is the difference between physical and mental love? —*Sixth-grade boy.*

How would you know if you were in love? Is it hard to tell? I mean, how would you feel? —*Fifth-grade girl.*

Why are people mean to kids? Sometimes I feel like running away. I think nobody loves me. They treat me like a dog. Every time I get hurt, people laugh at me. Only one person loves me, and that's me. Can you help me? —*Fifth-grade boy.*

Different kinds of love

"Love" is a short word that we use for lots of different kinds of feelings. Perhaps the first thing to understand is that love and sex are not the same. Love is a much larger set of ideas and feelings than sex. Sometimes people say they "made love" when they really mean "made sex"—that is, they had sexual intercourse or other kinds of close body contact. There's often lots of love in sex, but just as often there is not. We'll talk more about that in Chapter 4, the one on sex.

Aren't there lots of different kinds of love? I mean, you wouldn't love your sister the way you love your friend, or your grandparents, or your dog, or God, would you?   —*Fourth-grade boy.*

Yes, there are lots of different kinds of love. Here are some of the kinds people most often talk and write about:

Love of God: Most religious people have a feeling that they love God and that God loves them. They find that this love gives them strength and comfort and often joy. (A special name for it is "divine love.")

Love of all people: Some people feel a sense of unselfish love, concern, and respect for every person in the world. They even feel unselfish love for people who might be considered their enemies. Some people use the Greek word *agape* (ah-GAH-pay) to name this kind of love.

Self-respect or self-love: This is the feeling of most people that they are worth a lot simply because they are human beings. They respect themselves as individual people. It doesn't mean they are selfish, only that they know their own value. It's very hard for people who don't respect themselves to have much respect for others.

Family love: This is the love people feel for each other because they are members of the same family. It includes the love of parents for their children, and of children for their parents, and of brothers and sisters for each other. Often it extends to grandparents and grandchildren, to aunts and uncles and nieces and nephews, and even to others who become part of a "family," such as adopted children or very close friends.

Married love: This is the special love that people feel who are married to each other. They have promised to love and care for each other for the rest of their lives. In good marriages, it usually includes many kinds of love: family love, friendship, and sexual love.

Friendship: Love between close friends is a special kind of love. You are happy when you are with a friend. If it is a really good friendship, you trust each other and can talk about anything and everything.

Love of pets: The joy, comfort, relaxation, and pleasure that people feel with their pets—their dog, cat, possibly even fish—is a special kind of love. Sometimes you may even feel that the only creature in the world that loves you is your pet!

Sexual love: This is the love that two people feel for each other's bodies. It is a strong sense of physical attraction. A special name for it is *erotic* (ee-ROT-ick) love. (The word comes from the name Eros, who was the ancient Greek god of love.)

Obviously, there are even more kinds of love: love of knowledge, love of beauty, love of humor, love of sports, love of doing things well (achievement), love of money, love of power— you can make your own list.

Also obviously, different kinds of love get mixed with each other, and people can love each other and love life in many ways.

Now, I'll try to answer the questions boys and girls most frequently asked about love. As you will see, in many cases I've stated the best answer I can, but it may not be *the* answer. Therefore, I suggest that you discuss these questions with other people. Talking about them will increase your understanding.

What's the difference between like and love?   —*Sixth-grade girl*.
Some people use the two words as if they meant the same thing. For example, "Wow! He really likes her!" or "OK, I admit it. I like him." However, *liking* is generally not as strong a feeling as *loving*. You like someone you've just met; you like most of the

people in your class; you like a TV performer; you like dogs and horses. But you love your parents (most of the time!); you love your sisters and brothers; you love a very good friend; or you love somebody in a strong, deep, exciting way that you could call "being in love."

So if people say they "like but don't love," it means that they enjoy the other person but don't have as deep and strong a feeling for them as love.

How come when a boy really likes a girl his parents say it's puppy love? —*Sixth-grade boy.*

Most puppies seem to love everybody and anybody they meet. They jump around and are very friendly. They don't need any deep, long relationship in order to act in a loving way. That's why people use the term *puppy love* for the strong feelings very young people have for each other. It's not to say the feelings are bad, only that they are probably temporary and not very deep. This is not to say, however, that "puppy love" doesn't often feel deep and important to those who experience it. To say that would be an insult to the feelings of young people.

How do you get a boy to be friends? —*Sixth-grade girl.*
How do you make a girl like you? —*Fifth-grade boy.*
How do you approach a girl? —*Sixth-grade boy.*

A lot of boys and girls asked questions like these. They knew there was someone they liked, but from a distance, so to speak. They wanted to know how to get closer.

One of the risks of telling someone that you'd like to be friends is that the person may not be interested. The person may say, in effect, "No thanks" or "I really don't want you for a friend," or they may just ignore you. And that hurts.

But you have to take some risks in this world. Also, most people like to know that someone wants to be their friend. Therefore, probably the best advice is: Just go ahead and *say* you'd like to be friends. Then suggest something you might do together—sit together at lunch, go roller skating, join a group and go to the movies, watch TV, or whatever. Maybe the person will say no.

Okay, too bad. But try again a couple of times, and if it doesn't work, remember that there are lots of other people in the world.

As for "How do you *make* a girl or boy like you?"—you can't. A feeling of liking or loving can't be forced on another person.

Should it always be the boy who asks for a date?   —*Fifth-grade girl.*

A lot of people think so, and that's the way it used to be and still is in many places. However, things have changed a lot over the past several years. Many girls feel much more free to ask a boy out. And many boys are glad to be asked. So the answer to the question is *no.* Girls and boys should be equally free to ask—and to answer yes or no, or maybe.

Why do kids think it's love and sex when a boy and girl invite each other over to roller skate?   —*Fifth-grade girl.*

Because they're silly, or they like to gossip, or they believe something they read or saw on TV. Also, of course, a friendship that starts with roller skating, or any other enjoyable activity between friends, can develop into something deeper. But in fourth, fifth, and sixth grades, it usually doesn't. It's just a good way to have fun together.

How do you tell a girl you love her?   —*Sixth-grade boy.*
How do you tell a boy you love him?   —*Fifth-grade girl.*

An obvious answer is "Just tell him or her!" It takes some courage, though, because "love" can be a word with lots of deep meaning. Therefore, if people are old enough really to fall in love, and to date seriously, and maybe even to think about whether to get married, they should be careful before they say, "I love you."

And there are ways other than just "telling," with words. You can find ways to spend time together. You can "love" the way the person looks and what the person does, and you can say that to the person.

In fourth, fifth, and sixth grades, and on into junior high school, boys and girls generally are not ready to be in love in any heavy, lifelong way. But this doesn't mean that they don't have strong feelings of attraction to other people. Some do; some don't.

Probably it's best not to try to make any statement to the other person but just to get to know each other and enjoy each other's company.

What should you do if you like someone and they don't like you? —*Sixth-grade boy*.
How do you tell a girl who's crazy about you that you don't like her? —*Sixth-grade boy*.

It's just a fact that "liking" someone is sometimes a one-way feeling. It always has been and always will be—with boys and girls, and with men and women. So if you like a boy and he doesn't like you, you probably just have to accept the fact. That may be hard to do, but if you don't, you'll just seem like a pest to him. The same goes for a boy liking a girl. Of course, maybe it will change, but don't push it. Make other friends. Don't sulk. Be likable!

What about the other way round? You don't like the boy, but the boy likes you. How do you let him know that you don't like him? Well, you can just not show any interest and he will get the idea. But if that doesn't work, you will have to find a way to say something like "You're a nice person, but I don't have any special feeling for you. I just think you should know that."

It might make you feel better to know that in grades four, five, and six, it is quite unusual for girls and boys to really fall in love with each other and to do things as a couple. Groups of friends and acquaintances are much more usual, even though people often have two or three "best" friends. The love they feel for them is the *friendship* love I explained on page 43.

Does everyone fall in love? —*Fourth-grade girl*.

No. Some people never "fall" in love. Some people get to know another person, and *gradually* love develops. Some people have friends they love, family they love, and people they love because of the work they do together, but they don't "fall" in love.

A person's life can have lots of love in it without their ever falling in love.

Can you fall in love in one day? —*Fifth-grade boy*.

Yes, you can, and quite a few people do—even in one instant. That doesn't mean that, having fallen, they will stay in love forever.

But there are quite a few people who've been married for many years who say that they knew the moment they saw each other that "*he's* the one!" or "*she's* the one!"

On the other hand, it is more common for that first moment of "Wow!" to gradually develop into true love over a period of time. People make lots of mistakes if they feel "Wow!" and then, without thinking, have sex or decide to get married. I say more about this in the next chapter.

How do you know when you love somebody? —*Sixth-grade girl*.

This is an easy question to ask, but it's difficult to answer. However, a great many boys and girls asked it. Here are some answers:

You feel very strongly attracted by the way the person looks.

You can't stop thinking about the person and about the pleasure of being with him or her.

You feel very strongly attracted by the way the person acts, by his or her personality.

You love the way the person speaks and laughs and reacts to things.

You feel that, no matter what, you will stay with and support and help and enjoy the person.

Then there were a lot of questions that can be grouped under this question:

What does love do for you? —*Fourth-grade boy*.

A brief answer, but an important one, is that it often makes you feel happier, stronger, safer, more filled with joy and courage. Of course, to make you feel this way, it must be shared steadily with another person who loves you. It is unusual for such deep love to develop when people are in their early teens or younger— except, of course, for family love, and sometimes the love in friendship.

Does love do something to the mind? —*Fourth-grade boy*.

Yes, it does. It is difficult to think coolly and clearly about someone you love. People say, "Love is blind." They mean that you may be less likely to see the faults and weaknesses of a person you love. You love them, and they look and seem beautiful or handsome to you no matter what.

Is love funny sometimes? —*Fifth-grade girl*.

Yes, it is. Of course, it depends on what you mean by "funny." But people in love often see the funny side of things. They laugh together and sometimes laugh about each other. Many often laugh about the way life is. They even laugh—in a loving way—about the sad things in life.

Why do people supposedly feel something in their hearts when they fall in love? —*Fifth-grade boy*.

Love can be exciting. When people are excited, their hearts beat faster. They can feel their hearts beating faster. So for centuries people have put hearts and love together.

Why do you stutter and stumble over your own tongue when you try to talk to a person you might love? —*Sixth-grade boy*.

When people are excited and nervous, they sometimes have a hard time talking. When people want very much to make a good impression on other people, sometimes they get nervous. Perhaps it's like being nervous and shaky before an important test. People are afraid they'll do something foolish. That can make them stutter, or they may be so excited by the feelings of love that they stumble over their tongues.

Does love interfere with your work at school? —*Sixth-grade boy*.

It can. If you are in love, you may think so much about it that it's hard to think about schoolwork. Or if you're worried about love, that can hurt your schoolwork. But when people are mature enough to be really deeply in love with a love that lasts, that feeling usually makes it *easier* for them to work well and think well. It usually makes them stronger in every way.

Here are some more questions that boys and girls asked about love:

Can you love somebody and not get married?   —*Fifth-grade girl*.

Yes, you can. Sometimes people love someone who does not return their love. That's hard, but it often happens. That love would probably never lead to marriage. Also, there are people who love each other but decide that even though they are in love, they are not ready to marry. Sometimes they live with each other without being married. Many religions teach that this is sinful. In any case, there is no question that there are many people who are in love and not married.

Why do girls like to have babies when they are in their teens?
—*Sixth-grade boy*.

It's clear that there are teenage girls who like to have babies. Why? Well, they may see a baby as a little person they can love and who will love them, and they feel the need for that love. Also, they believe that having a baby will make them important and grown-up. They hope people will respect them because they are mothers. They can show off their cute little baby to their friends. They may hope that the father of the baby will marry them and they can have a family. In addition, when a girl is unhappy in her own family, if she has a baby, she may be able to get financial support from the government, enough to help her be independent of her family—to establish a family of her own.

But, of course, there's another side to the question. When they find out they are pregnant, many teenage girls wish they were not (and often the boys who made them pregnant feel the same way). How they got into this situation and what they should do about it are discussed in Chapter 4. In brief, though, they may have gotten pregnant because they did not know how to avoid it; or because they felt unable to say *no* to a boy or man who wanted them to have sexual intercourse with him; or because they did not know about birth control or forgot to use it. (See Chapter 5.) Once they have gone through the nine months of pregnancy and have given birth, they feel strongly attached to their baby. Therefore, it *looks* as if they "like to have babies." But, in fact, although they love the baby, many of them wish they had waited till they were older. The chapters on sex and families will answer some more questions about all this.

Why do people say, "I love you," when they don't mean it?
—Sixth-grade girl.

There are lots of different reasons. One is that maybe they think if they say "I love you," the person they said it to will like them better, or do something for them—buy them something, go with them on a date, have sex with them.

Maybe when they say it, they really *believe* they love the other person. But maybe it's just "puppy love." Maybe they just felt in a romantic mood and were "swept off their feet."

Maybe it just seemed like a nice thing to say, and they wanted to be nice or make the other person feel nice.

Maybe they didn't *really* say it, but the other person just thought they did. Sometimes people hear what they want to hear.

Maybe they just meant it lightly, as in "I just love you when you sing (or dance, run, play, talk, smile, frown, etc.) like that!" They mean it as a pleasant compliment, but the other person took it much more seriously.

Maybe they really *do* mean it, but then they don't act like it. Parents and children sometimes say, "I love you," and they really do; and yet a few minutes later they are shouting and scolding.

One thing is sure, though. If a person says *seriously* to a person, "I love you," and doesn't mean it, it's a lie. It's not treating the other person fairly or truthfully, and that is wrong and can damage both the sayer and the hearer.

And if someone says, "I love you," just to get something for him or herself, that is wrong. There's much more to love than *saying* it. But if love is real, it's good to say it.

How do you accept being dumped? *—Fifth-grade boy.*

"Being dumped" seems to be a common problem for fourth-, fifth-, and sixth-graders. They also see it happening to their teenage friends. It means that suddenly a person you like and who you thought liked you—or even loved you—won't have anything to do with you anymore. The person rejects you, and you feel "dumped," like garbage.

How do you accept it? First of all, nobody likes being dumped, so your feelings of sadness or anger, or that you are no good, are perfectly normal. It's no fun for anybody to be rejected by a person he or she likes. So accept your feelings as real and natural.

And then you just have to look around and think about all the people there are who like you and are you friends. Also, you know that millions of people like you have been dumped and lived through it—have even forgotten all about it.

Another thing: It may help to talk with a friend about it. Sharing your feelings often makes you feel better. In fact, once you're over the shock of being dumped, you may be able to talk with the person who dumped you. That person may be feeling bad too.

When you first love someone, will there ever be anyone better? *—Fourth-grade boy.*

Probably, but not always. A great many people "fall" in love quite young, even in grades four, five, and six. And that first love seems just amazing and wonderful. And it may happen quite suddenly. You see the other person and you are "stricken." That means that the feeling of love just hits you. But chances are, when you are young, that it's a love that won't last. It's just a wonderful new feeling, much more feeling than thinking. But when you test it out, and when you get to know the other person better, you will probably find after a while that the feeling wears off, or wears out. You and the other person both develop and change. She gets interested in hockey. You get all involved in science. He moves away, you stay, and after a few postcards, you are both absorbed in different lives. You have different experiences, and you grow apart. And yet that first feeling was wonderful, in some ways as wonderful as anything can be.

On the other hand, there are some people who fall in love only once. It may be when they are very young, or not until they are grown up and ready to marry. That once, whenever it happens, is *it*. And when, finally, these two people are ready to establish their lives together, there's no doubt in their minds. But, much more frequently, "when you first love someone," it's a delightful experience, and then both people move on and later have even better and deeper experiences.

Why does love end? *—Fifth-grade girl.*

Some love doesn't end—for example, the love of most parents for their children, the love of children for their parents, the love of many husbands and wives for each other, and the love of really deep friends.

But if loves does end, there can be many reasons why. Here are some. Do they fit any situations you know of?

Love only *seemed* to end. The people who loved each other got angry, or something terribly upsetting happened to them. But after a time, the trouble died down and the love was still there.

It wasn't really love in the first place. It was just *infatuation* (in-FA-chu-AY-shun), a feeling of attraction not based on anything important or lasting. Very often young people get infatuated with each other, and sometimes older people do too. It can even be fun to be infatuated, unless you do something that you will regret (become pregnant, or make a person pregnant; make deep promises that are broken; get married without thinking it out and without waiting to see how strong the feeling really is).

The people changed in some important ways. Sometimes people get too involved with their jobs and become unlovable; other times they begin to do terribly cruel, selfish, unloving things. Maybe one person starts to expect the other person to do all the unpleasant work, or falls in love with someone else. In other cases, one partner becomes an alcoholic and can't stop drinking even with help, or seems to stop having self-respect and becomes hopelessly messy and unattractive.

Sometimes conditions of life change in important ways that affect people's feelings. Examples: A person has to be away quite often for long periods of time; people suddenly become very poor or lose their jobs; children grow up and move away; a tragedy happens (such as fire, accident, or the death of a child) and shakes up the people who loved each other.

There's more about this question on pages 108–111, where I talk about divorce.

Why do people love each other for five years, and then get married, and then hate each other? —*Sixth-grade boy.*

It sometimes happens. All one can say is that the people must have felt that marriage would solve all their problems, and it didn't. Or they loved each other when they still felt free, but when they got married, they couldn't stand not being free. Or one felt that since they were married, one of them should do all the housework, or give up a job, and this was not acceptable to that other person. Or they got married because they felt they were drifting apart from each other and that getting married would stop the drift, and it didn't. (See the discussion on divorce, pages 108–111.)

Why do people who love each other fight? —*Fifth-grade girl*.

One might ask, "Why not?" It's only natural that people who live close to each other and who have to use the same things and space should get angry or disagree now and then. If they feel really close, they can feel free to argue, even to shout or to sulk. Probably any couple who say, "We've lived together for twenty (or five, or ten) years and never had an angry word," are not telling the truth. Or else they are so afraid their love won't last that they don't express their feelings. That's too bad—in most cases. Disagreements and fighting (*not* hitting, which is always dangerous to love) are a part of a life of love together. One of the mistakes children make is to assume that when parents fight together they really hate each other and that love has ended. And a mistake parents make is not explaining or showing their children that fighting and arguing—some of the time—doesn't mean they *don't* love each other.

However, when young people, such as teenagers, find that there is more fighting and arguing than there is enjoying and comforting and supporting, it's probably a sign that they're not really in love.

Perhaps by now I've answered, or at least given an opinion on, enough questions about love to help you figure things out better for yourself. You can see that the subject of love is complicated. Why not try talking about these questions and answers with other people? That's a good way to deepen your understanding of the subject, of other people, and of yourself.

Now here are three more questions fourth-, fifth-, and sixth-graders asked under the heading *love*. They lead well into the next chapter.

Is it harder to love somebody or to have sex with somebody?
—*Fifth-grade girl.*

Do people who love each other really have to have sex?
—*Fourth-grade boy.*

Do you have to love someone to have sex with them?
—*Sixth-grade girl.*

—4—

Sex

One fifth-grade boy commented on his questionnaire, "Sex is such a small word for a big meaning." How true! There are two larger words that say the meaning better. They are *human sexuality*. These words refer to all the ways we human beings act that are sexual, things we do that have to do with being male and being female. They mean much more than people touching each other's bodies and having sexual intercourse.

Many boys and girls asked, "Why is sex so important?" Some asked this, I think, because to them it is not important. They felt like the sixth-grade boy who wrote, "Sex: I have no problems with this predicament." On the other hand, most boys and girls make it clear that they know sex *is* important and want to know why.

One part of the "big meaning" the fifth-grade boy wrote about is what people mean when they talk about "having sex." They mean "having sexual intercourse" or "engaging in sexual intercourse." In Chapter 2, on human reproduction, you read how intercourse is the means by which human beings have babies—a penis enters a vagina, a sperm fertilizes an egg, and about nine months later, if nothing prevents it, a baby is born. Thus, "sex" is the way the human race continues to exist on earth. That's certainly important and big. But a man and a woman will not create a baby every time they have sexual intercourse, and they may not even want to. Later in this chapter, I'll explain more about sexual intercourse without creating babies.

In Chapter 2, you read that sex for reproduction and sex for good feelings are closely related but not the same. In this chapter, I

55

try to answer questions about sex for good feelings. Let's start with
the three questions at the end of the last chapter.

**Is it harder to love somebody than to have sex with some-
body?** —*Fifth-grade girl*.

Whoever wrote this question seems to feel that it's "hard" to
love somebody. Perhaps a better word would be "complicated."
Love is complicated, even though feelings of love can come
quickly. So the answer is: *Yes*, it's more complicated to love
somebody than to have sex with somebody. Having sexual intercourse, the physical act, is quite simple. Almost anybody can do it.
But, although the act is simple, the results and feelings are
complicated, as I shall explain in this chapter.

Do people who love each other have to have sex? —*Fourth-
grade boy*.

No. Obviously, people who love each other as members of a
family, or as friends, or as fellow human beings, do not have to have
sex. But, also, people who feel a sexual love for each other don't
have to have sex. It is a matter of decision about *when* to have sex
and *whether* to have sex. Many people decide not to have sex until
they get married. Others decide to wait until they are sure they are
deeply in love. Still others want to have sex whenever they have a
feeling of sexual love. Wise people, of any age, will think carefully
before deciding to have sex. They will also talk it over carefully
with the person they might have sex with, to be sure that they *both*
feel ready, and *are* ready. Many years ago, the Reverend Jesse
Jackson said to a large meeting of high-school students, "No
intercourse without discourse." (*Discourse* means exchanging
thoughts and ideas.) It was almost like a commandment from the
Bible. I think it was a good commandment, and still is. A sixth-
grade boy expressed part of the same idea when he said, "A man
and woman should consult before having sex. If they decide to
have it, they should take precautions before she finds herself
pregnant. If they don't, it's not fair to the baby." He's quite right.
But they should also take precautions with each other's feelings—
having sex with someone can bring about many complicated
feelings, as I've said, so both people should be certain they're
emotionally prepared.

Do you have to love someone to have sex with them? —*Sixth-grade girl*.

No, you don't have to. It is a fact that many people, young and old, have sexual intercourse without love. It would be untruthful to say otherwise. The more important question is: "*Should* you love someone before you have sex with them?" My own conviction is, yes, you should. I think sexual intercourse is too big an experience, with too many possible consequences, to be "had" without love. But this is something you will have to make up your own mind about.

Is sex something that should be thought about before doing? —*Fourth-grade girl*.

Yes! I hope you will think and talk about it carefully, at length, and well.

What is it like to have sex? Is it fun, or something to be serious about? —*Fourth-grade girl*.
Why do boys and girls have sex just to make them feel good? Why do they really take sex as a joke? —*Sixth-grade girl*.

There's no question that *if* two people both want to have sexual intercourse with each other, and *if* they both feel they are ready, and *if* they consider each other's feelings, having sex usually feels very good. (Note the three *if*s.) Thus, it is both fun *and* something to be serious about. But it's no joke.

Boys and girls who "take sex for a joke" and have it "just to feel good" may well get into lots of trouble: pregnancy, hurt feelings, sexual diseases, loss of respect from other people, bad feelings about what they did. If you think and talk about the problems, you'll doubtless be able to add to the list.

Why are kids embarrassed to talk about sex? —*Fifth-grade boy*.

It's probably true that most boys and girls are embarrassed to talk about sex. Part of the reason is that their parents are embarrassed to talk with their children about it. That may be because *their* parents were embarrassed to talk with *them* about it, and so on. The embarrassment is catching. In America, sex is generally considered to be a private matter. And when you suddenly talk about a private matter, it's embarrassing. For years I've taught sex education to junior-high-school students. At the beginning of every year, I find that when I ask the direct question "What is sexual intercourse?" nobody answers. There is silence, and then some smiles and giggles and poking. The students are, without a doubt, embarrassed. So it's perfectly normal to be embarrassed. It means you understand and feel what is expected of you in our culture. Our culture expects you to be embarrassed to talk openly about sex.

When I explain this to a class, and after they discuss it a bit, I answer the question about sexual intercourse, using the words *vagina* and *penis*. The roof doesn't cave in; nobody is struck dead. It's OK to talk! From then on, people are much less embarrassed.

A fifth-grader wrote, "Sex is a pretty private matter, after all." Yes, it is, and we should not forget this. Otherwise, we may offend people's feelings. One could say that our society is "sex-silent," as I've just explained. But it's also "sex-noisy." There's a lot of "noise" about sex on TV, radio, and records; at the movies, in magazines, and in advertising. And that's confusing to people—they see and hear about sex all the time, but nobody wants to talk about it.

Why are people so afraid to talk about sex? When someone is *not* afraid to talk about it, why do people laugh?   —*Sixth-grade girl*. When kids hear love or sex, they giggle. Where do they think they came from?   —*Fifth-grade boy*.

I've already answered these questions. I hope that reading this book will make you less afraid to talk about sex. It's a very important subject to talk about. We need discussion. And we need discussion not only about "where kids come from" but also about the feelings and choices and results involved in the sexual parts of our living and thinking: our sexuality.

Is sex dirty? If it isn't, why do people think it is?   —*Sixth-grade boy*.

It's a strange but common thing for people to think that sex is "dirty." When we talk about a "dirty joke" or a "dirty word," we usually mean a joke or word having to do with sex. But my plain answer to the question is: "*No*, sex is not dirty."

Perhaps one reason people start thinking that sex is dirty is that "down there" on our bodies, where some of our sex organs (our genitals) are located, are also located the openings from which we "go to the bathroom"—that is, from which we urinate and move our bowels. We are taught at a very young age to be careful to clean ourselves after using the bathroom. That's a good thing to learn. But it's important also to learn that urination and bowel movements are quite different from sex, which is, as I said, *not* dirty.

What is the age you should start liking boys? I sure don't like them yet. —*Fifth-grade girl.*
People are so eager for sex today, they tell you to get it as soon as possible. How do you tell when you are ready for sex? —*Fifth-grade boy.*
How old do you have to be to enjoy sex? I'm only eleven, but I think I would like to try it. Should I? —*Sixth-grade girl.*

There's no certain age when "you should start liking boys" (or girls). For many young people, other interests are much stronger—and this is true for many adults, too. And, of course, you can "like" boys or girls without having sexual feelings toward them at all. When one person likes another, sex isn't always a part of it.

But the girl who asked the question was probably worried that she was behind in her development. She felt she *ought* to be "liking" boys (having sexual feelings for them). That's a common worry. And the boy who says "people are so eager for sex today" is also probably worried. He's heard that he should want to "get it" as soon as possible. "When are you ready?" he asks.

No one answer will fit everyone. If you have to ask, seriously, "Am I ready?" you probably aren't. Take the girl who said, "I'm only eleven, but I think I would like to try it. Should I?" My answer to her would be: *No.* You're too young. It wouldn't be good to try. You probably wouldn't find it an enjoyable experience. And the risks are too great.

So how do teenagers tell when they are ready to have sexual intercourse. Asking themselves the following questions* may help

---

*These questions are adapted from an excellent book, *Reaching Your Teenager*, by Elizabeth Winship (Boston: Houghton Mifflin, 1983). Beth Winship is the writer of the column "Ask Beth," in the *Boston Globe* and many other papers.

them decide. A person is not really ready unless he or she can answer *yes* to all of them.

● Is your body really grown-up? Most people's bodies don't fully "grow up" until age seventeen or eighteen or later—even though most girls can get pregnant (and boys can make someone pregnant) several years earlier than that.
● Is your personality really mature? Do you have the self-control, patience, and understanding really to enjoy inter-course?
● Do you really know a lot about male and female sexuality? It's a complex subject, both the body part and the mental part.
● Are you strong enough to share your deepest feelings with another person? Are you able to share like that?
● Do you know about reliable birth-control methods—ways to keep from having a baby?
● Are you and your possible partner ready and prepared to *use* a birth-control method? *Knowing* is one thing; *using* is another.
● If, despite this, you get pregnant, or make someone pregnant, are you ready to take the consequences? They are never simple.
● If you get a disease from sexual contact with an infected person, do you know what to do? (I explain about VD—venereal disease—later in this chapter.)
● Are you sure you're not just trying to prove that you're mature? Having sexual intercourse doesn't prove a thing about a person's maturity, and it doesn't help make you mature. It's not anything to boast about, even though, as one sixth-grade boy wrote, "Everyone said they did it." He added, "I don't believe a word they say."

In animals, sexual intercourse or mating is usually referred to as *copulation* (KOP-you-LAY-shun). Perhaps the champion copula-tors we are familiar with are mice, rats, hamsters, or guinea pigs. If you try to prove something about yourself by how often you copulate, all you are proving is that you're a better copulator. You might as well be a guinea pig! It certainly doesn't prove anything about your quality as a male or female human being.

• Do you hope that having intercourse will *cause* the other person to love you? Are you *using* sex to try to *get* love? If someone says to you, "If you loved me, you'd have sex with me," it's *not* true. If he or she loved you, there'd be no pushing and urging to have sex before you yourself were fully ready.

• Do you really feel it's morally right for you to have sex? If you have doubts, of if you haven't really figured out what you believe, you're not ready.

The questions above concern readiness to have sexual intercourse. Having intercourse is not the only way to enjoy physical pleasure. On pages 66–67 and 86, I explain some of these ways.

I don't feel safe now and then. I feel funny—because I am growing black hair on my vagina. And soon under my arms. My mother said, "Honey, you're going to have to shave your legs soon." I am scared about growing up. What will I do? Will I ruin my life? Will I be the ugliest person in the world? —*Fourth-grade girl*.

Most people go through times when they don't feel safe. It is scary to grow up, not to be a little child anymore, to start having to be responsible for yourself and what happens to you.

When the signs of puberty come, it's a worry, too, for both girls and boys. (Look back at Chapter 2, pages 24 and 28.) Do you feel as if you're getting there too fast? Too slowly? It's intelligent to think about all this. It's normal—and it's tough to worry! So talk to your mother; talk to your father. Or talk with someone else whom you trust enough to share your feelings and worries with.

Will you "ruin your life"? A few people do. Most people now and then worry that they may. But if you think and plan and talk about your future, you almost certainly won't. And if you use the knowledge you have, and if you *respect yourself* as a person of worth (you're the only you in the world; you are of infinite value!), you won't. As for being ugly, have you ever listened to what a lot of people say when they see a photograph of themselves? They say, "What a terrible picture!" or "Gee, do I look like *that*?" But when you look at the picture of the person, it doesn't look terrible or ugly to you. Everybody feels self-conscious. Also, even if you aren't very beautiful or handsome, there's a lot more to you than your surface. There's the whole interesting you under the surface—your special unique personality, your sense of humor, your abilities and knowledge. And even the surface will change—and you can help change it—as you grow up. It helps to remember all this, even though it won't entirely stop your worrying.

What should you do if a boy tries something? —*Fourth-grade girl.*
I've been best friends with this guy for my whole life, and now he wants to get serious and do things I don't want to do. I want to say no, but I don't want him to lose respect for me. What should I do? —*Fifth-grade girl.*

The answer to both girls' questions is to say *no*. You don't have to say it as if the boy were bad. You can just say, nicely, "No. I'm not ready for that" or "I don't want to do that," and then, if you want, you can try to explain. It's certainly not your duty to say yes. Neither is it your duty to explain. But explanations often help, and can be reassuring to someone you're friends with. Remember about the importance of *discourse*!

And if a boy says, "But I *have* to!" or "I can't help it!" just leave him right then and there. Nobody "has to"; nobody "can't help it." Even if you *feel* like "doing something," you do *not* have to do it.

As for the boy "losing respect" for a girl who says no, he won't. There is absolutely nothing disrespectful about refusing to do sexual things you don't want to do or that you feel it's wrong to do. Keep that in mind as you grow through your teens—and through life.

Also, be sure that you yourself never put any other person under pressure to do something sexual that that person isn't entirely ready to do. Be sure that you both talk over everything well in advance. Talk, and wait—and talk again before you decide.

I'm very scared. What do I do if a boy should ask me where the bedroom is when I'm still too young (like about fifteen) to have sex? —*Fifth-grade girl.*

The answer is to say *no* and talk it over. And if he says, "If you don't, I won't love you anymore," it's a sure sign he doesn't love *you*. He may just desire your body, and you are much more than your body.

Boys ask questions like these too. For example:

If a girl liked you and you liked her and she offered to have sex with you, should you say yes? —*Fifth-grade boy*.
Girls seem to think some guys ought to have sex or they're just kids or babies. How do you keep a girl from putting you down? Do you have to have sex with her? —*Sixth-grade boy*.

Again the answer is: *No*—and explain. And if the other person laughs at you or suggests you're "just a baby," you can reply you're more than a body to have sex with. You are a whole person with many important feelings. Try not to be afraid to explain what you believe or what you feel. That's the way to be mature.

Kids around me tell me that they had sex with girls, but I don't. How should I answer when kids ask me if I had any sex? —*Sixth-grade boy*.

You can say, "That's *my* business" or "That's private." But if you have enough courage, tell the truth and talk about it. You may find that it gives others the courage to tell the truth too. It's a fact that people, especially boys and some men, tend to boast about how much sex they have—and half the time their stories aren't even true!

Both boys and girls asked whether it is wrong to *feel* that you'd like to have sex, but many more girls than boys asked it. The explanation is that by about age eleven, more girls than boys have developed strong sexual feelings. In two or three years, most boys "catch up," and their feelings become very strong too. In their early teens, more girls look and act and feel like grown women than boys look and act and feel like grown men. However, a girl's first menstruation usually (but by no means always!) happens about six months earlier than a boy's first ejaculation of semen. That is, the "average" girl can get pregnant only about six months earlier than the "average" boy can make a girl pregnant. Thus, as far as the ability to *reproduce* goes, girls are not as far ahead of boys as they look.

Is it wrong to want to have sex at this age—not have, but want? *—Sixth-grade girl.*
Is feeling a sexual attraction for a boy wrong, or is it just a part of life? *—Fifth-grade girl.*

To both questions, my answer is: No, it's not wrong. You can't control what you feel, but you must control how you act. It's quite normal to have sexual feelings, even well before you are really ready to have sexual intercourse. And it's also quite normal not to.

Sometimes I want to have sex, but obviously I am too young. This year I have had that feeling often. Also, I want to have sex before I get my period so that I don't get pregnant. Is this all right? *—Sixth-grade girl.*

To *want* to have sex, as I've explained, is all right. To know you're too young is intelligent and mature. But to try to have sex before your first period is dangerous. Some girls can get pregnant *before* they begin to menstruate.

Many, many boys and girls in fourth, fifth, and sixth grades want to know how sex feels.

Does sex feel good? Does it hurt when a guy is having sex with you? *—Fifth-grade girl.*

Yes, it does feel good *if* you *both* are ready for it—emotionally and physically. (Look again at pages 60–61 about what "ready" is.) But if a girl or woman is not ready to have intercourse, her vagina may be dry and tight, and when a boy or man forces his penis into her vagina, it will hurt her. However, if the woman is ready and her vagina is moist, it doesn't.

Also, the pleasant feelings during intercourse may include *orgasm* (OR-gazum). For both men and women (and boys and girls), an orgasm is a feeling of very intense pleasure—for this reason, it's sometimes also called a *climax*. In boys and men, orgasm takes place when they ejaculate.

I want to know: Does it hurt when we make love? Because some people make all kinds of noises as if it's killing them. *—Sixth-grade boy.*

The noises people make when they make love are usually noises of pleasure—*if* they are ready and can relax and enjoy themselves. But these noises may sound to other people like the noises of pain. However, if *force* is used, sexual intercourse can be very painful.

What is sex, really? All I know is that it is nasty stuff. What is it? *—Fourth-grade girl.*
On TV, people look like loving is really good. Is it? *—Fifth-grade boy.*
How does sex feel? Good? Bad? Refreshing? *—Fourth-grade boy.*

Sex can indeed be "nasty stuff" if it is *forced* by one person on another. But, as I've said, when two people know they're ready, it's quite the opposite and can be an expression of deep wonderful feelings.

Yes, on TV, sexual activity is usually made to look good. But remember, the people having sex on TV are *acting*. How you see them behave usually has very little to do with real life. Don't use what you see on TV to judge what sex is really like.

And how does sex feel? As I've said, it feels good if both partners are ready—and bad if they are not. Is it "refreshing" if it's good? In some ways, yes. For example, after they have sex, a happily married couple often feel relaxed, loving, close, content. But they may feel more sleepy and relaxed than "refreshed."

Does having sex make you more mature? *—Sixth-grade boy.*
No. However, having sex can deepen the love two mature people feel for each other.

Do people have to have sex to keep them comfortable? *—Sixth-grade girl.*
When people have a strong desire for sexual intercourse, a tension builds up in them and they may not "feel comfortable" until they have ejaculated or had an orgasm. *However*, the strong sexual desire people feel can be relieved by *masturbation* (MASS-ter-BAY-shun). Intercourse is not necessary. On the next page, I answer questions about masturbation.

Also, however, there are many people who say they never feel sexual tension. They never feel uncomfortable because of lack of sexual activity. And there are people who choose a life of *celibacy* (SELL-i-ba-see). That means a life without sexual intercourse or marriage. Catholic nuns and priests promise to be celibate because of their religious belief that a sexual relationship will interfere with their special closeness to God. They take vows of celibacy.

Also, as you know, there are many, many people who choose not to have sexual intercourse until they are married. They may do this for religious reasons or for personal reasons. These people may also feel sexual tension and a strong desire to have sex, but they stick by their decision to *abstain* (ab-STAYN) from—not have—sex until marriage.

People talk about "playing with yourself." What does that mean?
—*Fifth-grade boy*.
Is it OK to masturbate? (I do.) *—Fifth-grade boy*.
Can a woman do what they call "masturbate"? I know ways to make myself feel very good. *—Sixth-grade girl*.

"Playing with yourself" means touching your own body in ways that give you sexual pleasure. The standard word for it is *masturbation*. Little babies, both boys and girls, quite naturally touch their genitals and enjoy the feelings it gives them. Later on they learn, usually from their parents, that touching and rubbing yourself "down there" is something you should do only in private, not out in public, where people can see you.

A boy or man masturbates by rubbing his penis, either with his hand or against something. After a time, he has an orgasm. Many boys do not have orgasms until they reach puberty (see page 28), and then they ejaculate semen when they masturbate.

A girl or woman masturbates by rubbing her vagina, vulva, and clitoris (see page 21). The clitoris is a small bump of flesh that is full of nerve endings. They are quite a lot like the nerve endings in a man's penis. When a girl touches or rubs her clitoris, it grows harder. After a while, she will probably have an orgasm. As the sixth-grade girl wrote, it "feels very good."

Is it OK to masturbate? Well, it feels good. It does no harm to the body, either of a male or female. However, there are some religious groups which teach that it is not OK, that it is wrong and sinful. If you are taught that and masturbate anyway, you might feel bad about it.

(*Special note*: On page 21, I said that sex for reproduction and sex for feelings are not the same, even though they are closely related. A woman's clitoris is an example of a sexual organ that is not necessary for reproduction. If a female has reached puberty and has intercourse, she can become pregnant even though she may not have an orgasm or feel any pleasure. All that is needed is for a man to ejaculate semen into her vagina. Therefore, the clitoris is a sexual organ but not a reproductive organ. A man's penis, however, is both sexual and reproductive. He must eject sperm in order to make a woman pregnant.)

I had a wet dream some time ago. Why do they happen?
—Fifth-grade boy.

A "wet dream" is when a boy ejaculates semen during his sleep. This usually happens when he is having a dream about something sexual. All it means is that his body needs to get rid of surplus semen. It is perfectly natural. Boys are often embarrassed by the spots of dried semen a wet dream leaves on their pajamas and sheets. They don't need to be embarrassed. Their parents will understand what happened. For some boys, a wet dream is the first signal that they have reached puberty.

Sometimes when I am in bed my vagina and breasts get a funny good feeling. Is that abnormal? *—Sixth-grade girl*.

No, it's not abnormal. Some young teenagers have such a "funny good feeling" quite often. It's a part of their sexual nature. Others don't have such feelings till much later. Remember, people differ very much from each other both in the strength of their sexual feelings and in the age at which they begin to be aware of such feelings.

Some people say the greatest thing in this world is to have sex. Is that true? *—Fifth-grade girl*.

It's true that having sex is one of the greatest pleasures in life. This is true for people who are ready for it and mature enough to have and enjoy it under pleasant circumstances. On the other hand, when very young people have sex in a hurry—"just to have sex" without knowing each other well first—they usually report that it wasn't so wonderful. "You mean that's it? That's what all the fuss is about?" they ask themselves.

But under good circumstances, surrounded by love, is sex "the greatest thing in this world"? For some people, for parts of their lives, yes, it is. Even for these people, though, sex isn't all of life. It is only a part of a life that has much more than sex in it.

There are other people for whom sex is only one of many great pleasures, including also the pleasure of laughter, the pleasure of adventure, the pleasure of doing a good job on something important, the pleasure of talk with friends, the pleasure of religion, the pleasure of a new idea or a new understanding, the pleasure of doing well in sports, the pleasure of praise, the pleasure of a perfect meal—I could go on and on. So could you, no doubt, naming your great pleasures.

Perhaps the best answer, then, is that "having sex" when you and your partner are really ready for it, and when it is a part of love, is *one* of the greatest pleasures of life.

A number of boys and girls asked questions related to learning about sex in school, as a part of the school's program.

What is sex education? —*Fifth-grade boy.*
We do not have a sex-ed. class in our school. Why don't we?
—*Sixth-grade girl.*

Sex education is teaching boys and girls in school the information they need to make intelligent decisions about sex. It is teaching facts that any well-educated person should know. Often churches and other organizations where boys and girls meet also teach sex education, sometimes with parents helping out. Usually it involves teaching about the sorts of things that I have been explaining in this book. A great advantage of sex education in schools is that it gives boys and girls a safe chance to talk about and discuss the information they are learning. That helps them make good decisions about how to behave and act.

Most boys and girls, and from 75 to 85 percent of parents, are in favor of sex education in schools. So why do most schools not have it? Probably because some people are afraid that teaching about sex will cause young people to go out and try it. But there is no evidence that this is so. It's true that some young people try sex, but *not* because they learned it in school. It's because they feel like it, or they feel pressure to do it, or because they see it and hear about it so much on TV, radio—as well as in books and magazines.

Nobody ever teaches us about sex, so we learn off the streets. Do they want us to become sex maniacs? —*Fourth-grade boy*.

Well, obviously, no person who cares about kids wants them to be sex maniacs, to go wild about sex. It *is* better to learn about sex in a course at school, or from parents at home.

Why do parents tell you as little as possible about sex and then get mad when teenagers try it in order to find out? —*Sixth-grade girl*.

It's a good question, and one it might be useful to ask your parents or a teacher you feel free to talk to. Maybe you and your parents can help persuade your school to start a course in sex education. But why do parents tell their children "as little as possible about sex"? As I said, it's probably because they are afraid that if boys and girls are told about sex, they'll go out and try it.

I think they are wrong about this. Teenagers and younger boys and girls do find out a lot about sex. They learn it from TV, from radio, from records. A fifth-grade boy wrote, "Explain that love and sex isn't really what's on TV and in magazines. That's just acting and selling stuff." How true!

When boys and girls talk with each other about sex, often what they find out is just plain wrong, or only partly true. Then they go out and act on the basis of wrong information and get into trouble. That's another reason why we need sex education at home and at school.

Here are some wrong ideas that get passed around:

● You can't get pregnant the first time. Wrong! You *can*.
● You'll win a boy's respect, or a girl's respect, if you have sex. Wrong! You'll often *lose* it; and if that is why a person

"respects" you—because you'll have sex—the respect isn't worth having.

● If you don't have sex as soon as you feel like it, you'll lose your sexual power and abilities. Wrong! Your ability to have sex will last for many, many years even if you never have intercourse. When the right time comes, your power and ability will be there.

● You prove you're a "real man" or a "real woman" by having sex. Wrong! Almost anybody can have sex. It doesn't prove a thing about you except that you can have sex. It takes much more than intercourse to be a "real man" or a "real woman."

● If a man pulls his penis out of a woman's vagina before he ejaculates, she won't get pregnant. Wrong! Very often she will, because some sperms come out before he ejaculates. Also, very often a man gets so turned on by his feelings that he can't make himself pull out. He loses control.

● If you have sex standing up, the woman can't get pregnant. Wrong! She can get pregnant in *any* position.

● If you really love a person, you have to have sex because it's the best feeling and the best way to show love. Wrong! If you really love a person, you will talk and think very carefully together before you have sex. (See again the "Am I ready?" questions on pages 60–61.)

● If a woman urinates right after intercourse, she can't get pregnant. Wrong! Urine doesn't kill sperm. In girls and women, it goes out a different passage—the urethra. It doesn't come in contact with the sperm in the vagina.

I could make this list of wrong ideas much longer. The point is that you need a source of correct ideas and facts and a chance to talk about them. So it's good to ask your parents. It's also good to learn about sex in a sex-education course at school. Information doesn't cause trouble; it helps *prevent* trouble.

One other point: Many parents *do* talk with their children about sex. Once you get started, it's not so hard! On their questionnaires, lots of boys and girls wrote statements like these two: "In my family my father and mother say if I don't understand something I am able to ask freely. So I ask and they explain. I like this, for I have nothing at that point to be scared of or hide" (Sixth-grade boy); "I don't have many questions because I talk to my parents when I have questions, and they answer. So I know mostly everything" (Fifth-grade girl).

Another point: Often a book can help. For instance, if you and your parents read this book together and talk about it, it will make it easier to go on talking later when new questions come up.

Why is _Playboy_ improper for kids? After all, we have books written for us about sex. —_Fifth-grade boy_.

The trouble with _Playboy_ is that its pictures give the message that sex and beautiful bodies are the most important things in the world. This isn't true. Also, all those bodies are very carefully photographed to be glamorous; they give you the idea that a _Playboy_ sort of body is the only sort to have. That's not true either. Most people don't have such "sexy" bodies, and it makes some people feel bad about themselves to compare their bodies with those in _Playboy_. So it's bad sex education. Also, the magazine suggests that sex is just play. It's a lot more than that!

Do you think I should ask my teacher about people and love and sex? —_Fifth-grade girl_.

Yes, if you feel comfortable about doing it, or even if you have to work up your courage to do it. Very often, grown-ups (teachers and parents) are embarrassed to start up a discussion about sex. If you can help them by asking, they'll often be glad you did, and will be happy to answer your questions. If the teacher says, "Ask your parents. I'm not supposed to talk about that," ask why. And, then, do ask your parents. What the teacher said may make it easier. Or you can ask your teacher, "Well, who can I ask?"

I sometimes cannot understand some sexual words my friends use. How do I deal with this? What should I say? —_Fifth-grade boy_.

If somebody uses a word you don't understand—any word, sexual or otherwise—it's a good idea to say something like "What does that word mean? I may be dumb, but I don't know." In most cases, you'll probably get an answer.

But it's not always so easy to ask that about sexual words. This is because so many boys and girls don't dare admit there's anything about sex that they don't know. They seem to think that anybody who *is* anybody will know all about sex. This is nonsense, and you can often help people, including yourself, by asking. You'll be surprised how many people besides you don't know. They want to know, but they don't dare ask.

Of course, one problem about sex words is that people often use slang instead of standard words when they talk about sex. Both children and adults do this, but probably boys and girls more than adults. And slang words change. Some words I used as a kid might not be the words kids use today. That's why in this book I've followed the advice of the sixth-grade girl I quoted at the beginning of this book: "Don't use slang, like *boner* instead of *erection*."

So when you ask what a slang sex word means, it might be a good idea to find out what the standard word for it is. That's a good way to get a discussion started with your parents or teachers.

Why do people get mad if I say things they call 'four-letter words'? They're just words, aren't they? —*Fifth-grade girl*.

The answer is that some words aren't "just words." Words carry feelings with them. The feelings you and people your age may have about the four letters f u c k may be quite different from those of your parents or your grandparents or your teachers. The four letters aren't "bad" or "dirty" in themselves. But the feelings of shock or disgust or anger they cause in other people are bad. Saying a word to people—or even where other people can hear it, even though it wasn't said to them—can be like hitting them. The word shocks them and they feel bad. That's why, if you are a kind person and care about others, you are careful about the words you use, especially on such a sensitive subject as sex.

You may think, "But they shouldn't feel that way." Well, okay, but they do, and, as I've said, we cannot control our feelings, much less other people's.

People, as I've said, are often embarrassed to talk about sex. Sometimes even the *standard* words shock them a bit, so they use nonsexual words to express sexual ideas. Perhaps that answers the question of a sixth-grade boy who wrote, "Why do people say 'the birds and the bees' when they mean sex?"

Why don't parents tell you about their sex relationship in bed?
—Sixth-grade boy.

Most people feel that their own sexual lives are a private matter. In our culture, sex is private. This doesn't mean that we can't learn about it, and be educated in school about it, but we don't feel comfortable talking about what we *personally* do "in bed."

This is especially true about parents with their children. You should respect your parents' feelings about their own private sex lives.

What should you feel like if you see your parents having sexual intercourse? What should you do? *—Fifth-grade girl*.

Sometimes this happens. If a family lives in a very small house and has to share bedrooms, it will probably happen. Or if a child opens the parents' bedroom door without knocking first and waiting for them to say, "Come in," it may happen, even if all the child wanted was to get something, or ask a question, or join in any other part of regular family life.

So what should you feel? You'll probably feel surprised and shocked. What you see will probably not look very romantic or beautiful. (Remember, movies and TV aren't real life.) The feelings of love that are a part of sexual intercourse don't show themselves to outsiders. It may even look as if one parent is attacking another, even though it isn't so. Therefore, you can't help having strong feelings.

What should you do? Probably the best thing is just to say, "Excuse me," and leave the room. Then try to find a time the next day to talk about it—not the details, but how you felt. And your parents may tell you how they felt when you came in without knocking.

Some parents, though, may handle such a situation differently. If you came into their room, they might stop and say something like "It's OK, Jerry. Dad and I are making love. But when we make love, we like to be private. So please go out and close the door. We can talk about it later. OK?"

On the other hand, some parents might gasp and look embarrassed. Well, that's a common way to feel when somebody, especially your own child, sees you doing something very private, like having sexual intercourse. If you just understand that and leave the room, there's nothing you have to worry about.

A good rule in a house is that whenever people are in their bedroom with the door closed, someone who needs to come in should knock first and wait for a "Come in!" If no one says, "Come in," then, unless it's a real emergency, go away. If it's an emergency, knock louder!

An exception to the privacy rule is when boys and girls are having a party together in somebody's house. In that situation the rule should be "All doors open all the time." Closed bedroom doors at parties can get lots of people into lots of trouble—both because of what can happen and of what people may *say* happened.

I would really like to know if my parents still have sex with each other. My mom got her thing that makes babies taken out. Also, I don't know if my dad can still make sperm. How old are men when they stop making sperm and having sex? —Sixth-grade girl.

A lot of boys and girls asked questions like this one. If you feel comfortable saying it, you could ask, "Mom, maybe you don't want to talk about it, but I'd like to know. Do you and Dad still have sex together?" Probably your mom or dad would be willing to answer, and probably the answer will be, "Yes, we do, and we enjoy it." They may add, "But it's a private part of our lives." If they don't want to answer, just remember, it's a private matter and you should respect that.

Let's look at the question more closely. "My mom had her thing that makes babies taken out." Probably the mother had a *hysterectomy* (HIS-tauh-RECK-tuh-mee). That means her uterus was removed by surgery because of cancer or some other disease. Such an operation does not mean that a woman cannot enjoy sexual intercourse as much as ever. She still has her vagina and her feelings. Or the girl might have meant that her mother had her "tubes tied." This is an operation that women have so that eggs can't pass down the fallopian tubes and sperms can't go up them. It's called a *tubal ligation* (TOO-bull ly-GAY-shun). It does not interfere with the pleasure of intercourse. It means only that the woman cannot become pregnant.

A similar operation can be done on a man. His vas deferens

tubes are cut and tied so that sperms do not get into the semen that he ejaculates. This operation is called a *vasectomy* (va-SECK-tuh-mee). It does not interfere with the pleasure of sexual intecourse, but he cannot get a woman pregnant. Both vasectomy and tubal ligation are kinds of *sterilization* (STEH-ruh-ly-ZAY-shun), which is any process that makes it impossible to create babies.

The sixth-grade girl goes on to ask how old men are when they stop making sperm. There's no definite answer to this. Many men continue to make and ejaculate sperm well into their seventies, even eighties. Some lose interest in sexual activity well before that, but many never lose interest in sex at all. It is almost certain that the father of a sixth-grade girl, unless he fathered her very late in life, can still make sperm.

When do women stop being able to have babies? Does that mean they stop having sex? —*Fourth-grade girl.*

Women reach a fairly definite time in their lives when they stop ovulating. It's called *menopause* (MEN-oh-paws) and generally comes sometime between ages forty-five and fifty-five. This means that a woman's ovaries no longer send out eggs to be fertilized. It does not mean, however, that a woman loses interest in sexual intercourse—only that she can no longer become pregnant.

Can old people have sex and make babies, or do their reproductive systems wear out? (By old I mean sixty and over.) —*Fifth-grade boy.*

I'll answer this question just to be sure we've made things clear. Yes, older people can have sex. However, by age fifty-five, almost all women have stopped ovulating and menstruating, so they cannot have babies. On the other hand, most men at that age still make sperm and *can* make a woman pregnant. People's reproductive systems don't "wear out." They just stop operating—men's generally at a much later age than women's. "Wearing out" suggests that if sexual and reproductive systems get used too much they wear out. They don't.

Why do girls get an abortion? Is it bad for your health to get an abortion? —*Fifth-grade girl.*

Why do people have sex and then kill the child before it is even born? —*Fifth-grade girl*.

A woman or a girl gets an *abortion* (uh-BORE-shun) because she has become pregnant and doesn't want to have a baby. You can figure out reasons why she would not want to have a baby. These are some: She doesn't want to interrupt her education or her job; she doesn't feel ready for the responsibility of being a mother; she already has as many children as she can take care of or has money to support.

If an abortion is done in the first three months of pregnancy, it is not bad for a woman's health. It is a minor operation. But it must be done by a medical expert at a clinic or hospital. If it is done by anyone else, or if a woman tries to do it herself, it can be *very* dangerous.

Obviously, abortion is a very poor method of birth control, of avoiding having a baby. It's much better to use a *contraceptive* (con-tra-SEP-tiv), or not to have sexual intercourse at all until the couple is ready to have and care for a baby. Contraception is explained on pages 77–79.

Now to the question "Why kill the child before it is even born?" The big question is: Is the embryo or fetus a *child*? (Remember, an *embryo* is the growing organism during the first four months of pregnancy; after that it's called a *fetus*.) The U.S. Supreme Court said in 1973 that it is not considered a *person* until it is born. Therefore, having an abortion is not "killing a child." And many women (and men, too) think that a pregnant woman should be allowed to choose for herself whether or not to have a baby.

However, many other people believe very strongly that the embryo or fetus has a "right to life," and that no one has the right to destroy it. They point out that once the egg and sperm have met and the zygote starts to grow, it is an individual, no matter how small, and that it is not a part of its mother's body. It just gets nourishment from her and a place to grow (in her uterus).

People argue passionately on both sides of this question: Is abortion killing a child? Does a woman have the right to choose an abortion? It's a question about which you'll have to make up your own mind.

When boys and girls have sex, do they always have a baby?
—*Fourth-grade boy.*
What do people do so they can have sex and not have children. —*Fifth-grade girl.*
For future reference, I would like to know how dangerous birth
control pills are. How well do rubbers work? How many times do
you have to have intercourse in order to have a kid? —*Sixth-
grade boy.*

No, when men and women (or boys and girls) have sex, they
don't always have a baby. They avoid having a baby by using *birth
control.* That means using some method of *contraception* (CON-
tra-SEP-shun). There are many methods of contraception, but they
all have the same purpose: to keep a sperm from meeting an egg
and fertilizing it. Here are some of the methods:

- *Birth-control pills ("the Pill"):* These pills stop a woman
  from ovulating. Therefore, there is no egg to be fertilized. If
  used exactly according to instructions, the Pill is not dangerous. It does not cause cancer. Taking one or two pills before
  having intercourse is useless and will not provide birth
  control. The Pill must be prescribed by a doctor.
- *IUD (Intrauterine Device) (in-tra-U-tuh rinn):* This birth-
  control device also must be prescribed by a doctor, who places
  it inside a woman's uterus. An IUD works by preventing the
  fertilized egg from implanting itself in the lining of the uterus
  and thus growing into a baby. This method should not be used
  by very young women.
- *Diaphragm (DY-uh-fram):* This is a rubber cap that a
  woman inserts in her vagina before intercourse so that it
  blocks the cervix (and therefore sperms cannot get into the
  uterus). It is used with a special cream that kills sperms. A
  diaphragm must be prescribed and properly fitted by a doctor
  (different women wear different sizes).
- *Contraceptive sponge:* This small plastic sponge contains
  spermicides (chemicals that kill sperms). A woman puts it into
  her vagina, against the cervix, before she has intercourse.
  These sponges, which can be bought without a prescription,
  must be used exactly according to the instructions on the
  package.

- *Condom (CON-dum):* This device is a soft finger-shaped piece of rubber that is fitted over the erect penis before intercourse. It prevents the sperms from getting into a woman's vagina, by holding them inside a small pocket left at the tip. If it isn't used carefully, according to package directions, it doesn't work. It is often called a "rubber" and can be bought without a prescription. If the woman uses a sperm-killing jelly or foam at the same time, this method can be very reliable.
- *Jellies, creams, and foams:* These are sperm-killing substances that a woman puts into her vagina before intercourse. They can be bought without a prescription, but they aren't very effective when used alone; it's best if the man uses a condom at the same time.
- *Natural family planning (NFP):* This method involves no special devices. Instead, a woman learns how to tell when she is going to ovulate. Then she can refrain from having intercourse for several days before and after ovulation (the time when she is most likely to get pregnant). Generally, a woman takes an NFP training course, which teaches her how to: (1) study the texture of her vaginal mucus, which changes at different times in her menstrual cycle, (2) keep track of her temperature, which rises just after she ovulates and stays up until she's about to ovulate again, (3) feel the position of her *os* (OSS), the opening in her cervix, and (4) record the pattern of her menstrual periods on a calendar. (A calendar alone is not reliable, since most women's periods are never perfectly regular. Some women try to guess the time of ovulation based only on such a calendar; this is called the *rhythm* method, and it is not effective.)
- *Withdrawal:* In this method, the man withdraws his penis from the woman's vagina before he ejaculates. It is not a reliable method, because sperms often leak out of the penis before ejaculation.
- *Sterilization:* If a man or a woman is sure that he or she never wants to have any more children, this is the method often chosen. It involves a surgical operation performed by a doctor and is generally permanent. When a woman is ster-

ilized, her fallopian tubes are cut and blocked so that no eggs can meet sperms. In a man, the vas deferens tubes are cut and blocked, and there are thus no sperms in his semen. Both women and men can continue to have sex as usual, with just as much pleasure, after sterilization.

It's very important to know that, except for sterilization, no method of contraception is 100 percent reliable. And, to answer the sixth-grade boy's question, you might have to have intercourse only *once* to "have a kid," if the contraceptive method doesn't work. For young teenagers, and many older unmarried young people, too, the most certain method of birth control is not to have sexual intercourse. That's called *abstinence* (AB-stih-nence)—to abstain from intercourse.

Where can boys my age get contraceptives without my parents knowing, or without being embarrassed by people in the store or the druggist? —*Sixth-grade boy*.

You already know that my conviction is that for people in their early teens or younger, having sexual intercourse is risky and not a good idea. However, if you aren't convinced of that, and if you are going to have sexual intercourse, it's better to be protected from getting someone pregnant or becoming pregnant than to have sex and have an unwanted pregnancy. (The pregnancy is the responsibility of *both* the boy *and* the girl.)

So where do people get contraceptives? They can get condoms, jellies, foams, creams, and sponges from a drugstore. They can also get them from a branch of Planned Parenthood, which is listed in the telephone directory. The people at Planned Parenthood will strongly urge young teenagers to talk over the matter with their parents, but they will sell contraceptives to these young people if they insist, and will give careful instructions on how to use them.

Finally, as mentioned above, birth-control pills, IUD's, and diaphragms are available only from a doctor and cannot be used effectively without his or her guidance. Natural family planning requires proper training from a clinic or other health center.

I repeat, though—fourth-, fifth-, and sixth-graders should

know that they are too young to have sexual intercourse. The information I've given here can be used when you are old enough to pass the "Am I ready?" test on page 60.

Why do people make love without birth control when they don't want kids?   —*Fifth-grade girl*.
There are a number of reasons:

- They don't know about birth-control methods.
- They know about them but don't use them properly.
- Even though they use them properly, they still cause a pregnancy because the method isn't 100 percent reliable.
- They are so eager for a moment of pleasure that they just go ahead and forget the consequences. This is totally irresponsible.
- They believe contraception is morally wrong, so they just hope they won't cause a pregnancy.
- They know about contraceptives, but at the last moment they forget to use one.
- They are in a hurry and don't take the time to use the contraceptive correctly.
- They fail to talk about the matter ("No intercourse without discourse"!), and each one assumes the other one has taken care of matters (or one tells a lie and says it's taken care of).

If you have sex and get pregnant, are you to blame for it?
—*Fifth-grade girl*.
Yes, you are.
The only exception would be if you are forced against your will to have intercourse. That's called *rape*.

What is all this rape, anyway?   —*Fourth-grade boy*.
Why do men go around raping women and hurting them?
—*Fifth-grade girl*.
Rape is forcing sexual intercourse on a person who doesn't want to have it. It is a violent crime, using sex as the weapon. Most rapists are young men and their victims are usually young women. (Sometimes children are raped; so are helpless old women.)

Why do men rape women? Most rapists feel full of hate and want to hurt people. It isn't usually because they're feeling sexual desire. Often, they feel especially hateful against women and use rape as a kind of "punishment." Some men (and boys) become rapists in a group, thinking they're showing each other how "macho" they are. They see an attractive girl or woman and persuade themselves "she's asking for it." This is nonsense. People don't ask to be forced and hurt.

What should you do to keep from being raped? I mean, is there anything you can do? —*Sixth-grade girl.*

You should be careful not to go by yourself in places that are lonely and dark, like city streets and parks, without other people around. You should never get into a car with a stranger. You should not let a person into your house, or anybody else's, unless you are sure who that person is and unless you trust that person. Most rapes take place in houses or apartments, not outside. If you are being followed by someone you don't know, or someone you know but don't trust, go as quickly as you can to where other people are, to where it is well lighted. Run there if you think you should. Keep aware of what is going on around you.

If you don't want to have sex, what should you do if the person forces you? —*Fifth-grade girl.*

This is a hard question to answer. So much depends on what the situation is. Say clearly, "No, I don't want to have sex with you" or "No, I don't want you to do that, so please stop." Then, if you can, get away and go to where other people are.

If a person is stronger than you, or has a weapon (a knife or a gun) and your life is in danger, try to *talk* to the person. Persuade him to stop. Make him realize you are a person.

Shout or scream if there is somebody to hear you—but *not* if you think the boy or man may hurt you badly. Then you just have to try to keep talking and looking for a chance to get away.

If you are raped (forced to have sex), when it's over, be sure to tell someone about it as soon as you can—probably your parents. If they aren't available, tell someone else. They then should tell the police so that the rapist can be prevented from hurting other people. Also, you should see a doctor to make sure you haven't been harmed and to find out whether you are pregnant.

Why do some girls go along with being raped?   —*Fifth-grade boy.*

No girl "goes along with" being raped. She may seem to go along because she's scared not to, or because she's forced to. Or maybe she thinks if she does go along, the boy will then love her, and she wants that, not the sex.

One other thing: Later, a boy may tell other people that the girl enjoyed it, or encouraged him, when really she hated it and felt forced, felt raped.

What happens when you are sexually abused? What does it mean? What should you do?   —*Fourth-grade girl.*
I really need to know what this sexual abuse thing is. This is secret, but I have a relative (older) who comes to our house, and he gets me to sit on his lap and stuff. Sometimes he gives me candy, and I like candy. I guess I don't mind what he does. It doesn't feel bad, but it feels funny. (THIS IS SECRET!) I want to tell him to stop, but I don't dare, because he's a nice uncle. But he might get mad. What should I do? I don't want to get into trouble.   —*Fourth-grade girl.*

Back on pages 13–14, I explained that some children are abused—badly mistreated in several ways: They are hit and knocked around; they are abused with insults and shouting, or with serious teasing and nasty laughter. When they are abused in these ways, it's not their fault and they need to try to get help.

Another kind of abuse is sexual. Quite often, the young person is persuaded to do sexual acts with an older person by words or by offers of candy or money or other things the child wants. Usually, the abused child is told to keep everything secret—or else! And the child is usually scared to tell what happened, like the fourth-grade girl above. The child, or young person, often thinks that it's her or his fault. *It is not!* No matter how sexually attractive the young person may be or seem to act, it's not the child's fault.

If you are sexually abused, or if a relative or friend tries to touch you on your sexual parts and tells you to keep it secret, say *no.* Do not let yourself be alone with that person. Also, *do* tell someone you trust about it—preferably your mother or father, or both—so they can help you. If you are abused by a parent, tell someone outside and try to get help.

Also, if an adult asks you, or tries to get you, to touch him or her sexually, don't do it. Simply say quite positively that you don't want to. And then leave the person. Don't stay alone with him or her.

People who touch children on their sexual parts are called *molesters* (mo-LESS-ters). They *molest* children. Molesting children is a kind of sickness, and molesters need help.

Let's be sure what I've said is clear:

- *Don't* allow a person to: take off your clothing in a secret or sexual way; touch your sexual parts (your penis, your vulva, your breasts); kiss you in a sexual way; get you in a car with him or her or get you to go to a lonely place.
- *Do:* tell your parents if anything like this happens.

If it's one of your parents who is sexually abusing you, tell your other parent or someone else, no matter what.

If necessary, say, "*no!*" or "I don't like that!"; or just get away from there. If you have to, scream or kick or hit. But usually all you have to do is to say *no* and go away.

One other thing, however: If a child is sexually abused, it doesn't mean the end of the world for him or her. It has happened to lots of young people, and they do get over it and go on growing up normally and happily with no more problems than anyone else has. This is especially true if the young person knows that it was not his or her fault, and also has a chance to talk about it.

Why do older brothers and sisters like to touch younger brothers and sisters in places where they should not touch them? —*Sixth-grade girl.*

Usually it's probably just teasing, and you can just say, firmly, "Cut it out!" or "Quit that!" Or you can find a time and tell your brother or sister that you really don't like it. He or she may not even known how uncomfortable it makes you feel.

If that doesn't work, or if you think your older brother or sister is trying to molest or abuse you sexually, tell your parents and let them deal with it. If it doesn't work, tell them again. Remember, it's *your* body! You have a right to decide who's going to touch it and how. Nobody has a right to force any kind of touching on you.

Should a family's brothers or sisters have sex together?   —*Fifth-grade boy*.

No, never.

(*Special note:* All this talk about sexual abuse may make you think, "Gee, you mean we can't even hug and kiss each other in our family?" No, of course I don't mean that. Good, warm, loving hugs are a wonderful part of the lives of many families, and so are family kisses. It's nice to snuggle up to people you love as a part of your family, especially your parents and grandparents. It makes you feel comfortable and happy, and even stronger sometimes. This kind of hugging and touching is especially important for small children. Sometimes when children get into their teens, they aren't so enthusiastic about family hugging and kissing anymore. They get to feel pretty private about their bodies. That's OK, too.)

If two boys or two girls have sex, what do you call that?   —*Fifth-grade girl*.

When two people of the same sex—two men or two women—have sex with each other, the word for it is *homosexuality*. (*Homo* comes from the Greek *homos*, meaning "the same," *not* from the Latin *homo*, which means "man.") A homosexual person is one who is attracted to people of the same sex. Female homosexuals are often called *lesbians* (LEZ-bee-uns), a word that comes from the Greek island Lesbos. There, in ancient times, women enjoyed a homosexual way of life together. Both male and female homosexuals are often called *gay*, a word that came from the word meaning "happy and carefree." Gay love is thought by some to be carefree because it's just for pleasure. No children and family responsibilities come from it.

People who are attracted to members of the opposite sex are called *heterosexual* (HET-uh-ro, from the Greek *hetero*, meaning "different"). They are often called "straight," as distinguished from "gay." Then there are some people who are sexually attracted to members of both sexes. They are called *bisexual* (from the Latin *bi*, meaning "two").

Is there a homosexual stage that most kids go through? *—Sixth-grade boy.*

Many—but not all—boys and girls do go through a period before puberty and in their early teens of preferring the company of people of their own sex. And many of them do some sexual experimenting with friends of the same sex. For most boys and girls, this is a brief stage. For some, however, perhaps 5 to 10 percent, it is the beginning of a lifelong sexual attraction to people of the same sex.

Why do people turn gay and love other men? *—Fourth-grade boy.*
Why do people want to be gay, and what does being gay do to your life? *—Fourth-grade girl.*

Nobody knows why some people are homosexual, or gay. There are several theories: One is that they were born that way; another is that it has to do with how they were brought up in their very early years, well before 5 years old—but nobody knows. One thing is quite sure: For many people, it is not a matter of choice. They *are* gay or they *are* heterosexual, regardless of what they might *want* to be.

What does being gay "do to your life"? It depends on the person. One could as well ask, "What does being straight do to your life?" Many gay males and lesbians live very happy, successful lives. However, since a lot of people believe that it is bad and sinful to be gay, they make life difficult for gay people. It's harder for gay people to get some kinds of jobs. It's harder, without marriage and children and an ordinary family, for them to fit into everyday life. Many people feel uncomfortable being friends with gay men and women. However, more and more people these days understand that gay people and straight people all are human beings with the same rights and abilities and pleasures and problems.

Is it true that different people have sex in different ways? *—Fourth-grade girl.*

Yes, it's true. Just as people talk with each other in different ways; enjoy each other in different ways; laugh, scold, praise, bore, and stimulate each other in different ways; so they "have sex" in different ways. That is, they have intercourse in many ways and positions. They learn about those by talking with each other and trying out various ways to find out what gives them the most pleasure.

There are also ways other than sexual intercourse to enjoy sexual or other good physical feelings. One is masturbation. I've already explained that on pages 66–67. Other ways range from holding hands, to kissing, to stroking each other's hair, all the way to touching and feeling the most sensitive, private parts of each other's bodies.

I hear you can get diseases from sex. Is that true? —*Fifth-grade boy.*

It is true that you can get a number of diseases from sexual activity. Some of them are very serious. Most of them can be cured with the right medicine. These diseases used to be called *venereal* (vuh-NEE-ree-ul) *diseases,* or VD. (The word *venereal* comes from Venus, the name of the ancient Roman goddess of love.) A more accurate, newer name for them is *sexually transmitted diseases,* or *STD's.* These diseases are passed (transmitted) from one person to another by sexual activity, through the mucus in their mouths or private parts. This means not just by way of intercourse but also through deep kissing and other intimate sexual activity. Remember, it isn't "having sex" that causes the diseases; it's having sex with a person who has an STD, just the way kissing doesn't cause colds, but kissing a person who has a cold may transmit the cold germs to you and you'll get a cold too.

There are about a dozen common STD's. The five most common are *gonorrhea* (GON-uh-REE-uh), *trichomonas* (TRICK-uh-MO-nuss), *herpes* (HER-peez), *NGU,* and *syphilis* (SIFF-uh-lis). I won't explain them here, for they are complicated. The most important thing for you to know is that if you think you might have an STD, go at once to a clinic or doctor for treatment. Don't wait. Also tell anybody you have had sexual contact with so that he or she, too, may go for treatment. Proper treatment can almost always cure an STD, usually quite quickly.

If you don't have an STD treated and cured, it can result in great pain, arthritis (crippling damage to your joints), sterility (inability ever to have babies), other kinds of serious damage to your body, and sometimes death. Also, STD's can do great harm to a baby born to a woman who has one of these diseases.

And what are the main signs of STD's? They are: a burning feeling while urinating; irritation of the rectum, itching of the sex organs, small pink growths on and around the sex organs; a painless rash (spots) on hands or feet; any unusual bleeding or discharge from the vagina or penis. Often the symptoms of STD's are mild, hardly noticeable. So if you have any reason to think you might have caught an STD, you should go to a clinic or see a doctor. A boy who catches gonorrhea will know he's been infected, because it becomes very painful for him to urinate. However, a girl may have gonorrhea without any symptoms at all. Even if a boy with whom she had sex tells her he has gonorrhea, she may think, "Oh, well, I guess I didn't catch it." But she probably did. Thus, both sex partners should be tested and, if necessary, treated, even if one of them has no symptoms.

A man and a woman who have sexual intercourse or other sexual activity only with each other, and who do not have any STD, are very unlikely to get such a disease. The people who should worry about STD's are those who have sex with an infected person or those who have sex with several people they don't know too well. Sometimes a person does not tell another person he or she has an STD but goes ahead and has sex anyway. That is a very selfish, dangerous thing to do.

Young people who think they may have an STD should tell their parents right away, and go to a doctor or clinic. If they can't tell their parents, they should call the VD Hotline. It's toll-free and confidential. They will tell you where to go to be treated. They will not ask your name; they'll just give you information. The number is 1-800-227-8922 (if you're calling from California, 1-800-982-5883).

What is this herpes people talk about so much? —*Sixth-grade girl.*

Herpes is a common STD in the U.S.A. When you have it, the symptoms are painful little open sores, usually around the genitals. Herpes sores heal themselves in about ten days, but then they come back, again and again. The disease is not dangerous to the life of the person who has it, but it is very uncomfortable and very easy to spread to someone else. Also, if a pregnant woman has open herpes sores around her vagina, her baby will get the disease as it is born, and it will cause very serious problems for the baby. Doctors have not yet found a cure for herpes.

(*Special Note*: There is another STD that has only recently been discovered. It is called AIDS. People who have AIDS almost always die, because their bodies lose the power to fight off diseases—including serious ones, such as pneumonia. AIDS affects mainly homosexual males, and drug addicts who use hypodermic needles to inject themselves. At the time I write, no cure has been found for AIDS, but doctors are working very hard to find one.)

Are people just trying to scare us off sex by all this stuff about VD? —*Sixth-grade boy*.

No, they are not. As you've just read, all sexually transmitted diseases are a really serious matter. Therefore, you should know the facts, not just be "scared off sex."

It's true that a number of years ago, some people printed books with horrible pictures of people with syphilis sores and parts of their bodies destroyed by disease. They seemed to be saying, "Don't have sex or here's what will happen to you!" But today syphilis is easily cured if you get treated, and it does no damage if you get treated as soon as you have any symptoms.

So don't be scared. Be informed, and act intelligently.

What are whores and prostitutes? —*Fifth-grade boy*.

Prostitutes (PROS-ti-toots) are people who are paid by others to have sex with them. They sell their "sexual services." Most prostitutes are women, but there are also some men who sell sexual services, usually to homosexual men, sometimes to women. A *whore* (HORE) is a female prostitute.

Some prostitutes work alone; they are often known as "call

girls." Others work in a *brothel* (BRAW-thul), or whorehouse, where men come to have sex with them in exchange for money.

In most parts of the United States, prostitution is against the law.

Why do people want to be prostitutes? —*Fifth-grade girl.*

People are prostitutes because they want to earn money. They are willing to use their bodies to get money. For most prostitutes, having sex is just a job.

Some people really don't want to be prostitutes, but they can't find any other way to support themselves and their families, and they have to earn money.

Then there are young girls and boys who, for some reason, run away from home. They get lost and hungry and don't know what to do. They are picked up, fed, housed, and helped by adults who then make them sell their bodies for sex—they become prostitutes. Once they have gotten started on prostitution, and it's the only way they know to make money, it's hard to stop. These young people need help or they will ruin their lives. They especially need to get back to their families and start solving the problems that made them run away.

Before we get to the chapter on families, I should answer some questions that many, many boys (and a few girls) asked about dates. They are questions that have to do partly with sex, partly with love, and partly with how people get along with each other.

If you have got a girl on a date, what do you do? (I don't want to be a failure.) —*Fourth-grade boy.*

There's no single answer to this question. A date is a meeting between two unique people. Both people have feelings and ideas. There are things they enjoy doing, and things they don't enjoy doing. So a very good idea is to talk about what you'd both like to do. For young teenagers, it's a lot easier, and often more fun, to do something with a group of people—maybe go to a party; get together with a few friends at somebody's house; go skating; go to a movie—whatever you both would enjoy.

Be sure you let your parents and your date's parents know

where you are going, how you are going to get there, what you plan to do, how you are going to get home, and what time you will get home.

Nobody wants to be a "failure." If a date doesn't work out well, and you or your date don't have fun, that's too bad. But it doesn't mean you're a failure. Talk about it and agree on what to do next time. Or look around for another person to date. Nobody succeeds all the time!

How do you get related with girls? When you think you love somebody, do you always have to have sex? —*Fifth-grade boy*.

You get "related with" girls the way you do with any person. There's no magic way. You talk, you do things together (maybe just walk down the hall together at school; maybe sit next to each other in class, or on the school bus; maybe have a soda after school). You find out whether you enjoy each other's company.

If you "think you love somebody," no, you don't have to have sex. You might hold hands, or put your arms around each other, or kiss each other, just to see how it goes. But don't have sexual intercourse; that should be way down the road. How do you know if you're ready to have sex? Read again—maybe together—the questions on page 60 that help you know when you are ready for sex. Those questions, and your answers, will help you and your date decide.

Do you always have to go out and charm girls with food and gifts just for sex? —*Fifth-grade boy*.

Of course not! You and your date might enjoy giving each other gifts now and then. It's fun, too, to eat food together. But to give a person food and gifts in order to get sex is like paying for sex. The word for that is prostitution (see page 88). Enjoy food, enjoy gifts. But you should think and talk about sex as a much more serious thing.

To kiss a girl, do you ask her or go ahead and do it? What do you do, take her on a walk and then kiss her? —*Fourth-grade boy*.

Again, there's no one way to do it. Some people like to be asked and to talk about it. Some people just know by the way they feel and the way the other person feels—by the way they move and look at each other—that it would probably be okay to kiss. Whatever you do, do it gently; don't use any force; and if your kiss isn't welcome, stop.

Yes, one way is to "take a walk and then kiss her." However, it may be that she'll take you for a walk and she'll kiss you. These days it's not always the boy who makes the first move. A lot of boys are timid and even afraid. They're scared they'll be rejected. So are girls. That's why some good talking is so often the best way to find out how you both feel.

When you try to get started with a girl, why do they back off if they really like you? *—Sixth-grade boy.*

A girl backs off because she doesn't feel ready for sexual contact. She may not even feel ready to hold hands or do any touching. She may think—maybe because of past experience or what's she's heard—that a kiss will lead to other body contact and maybe to a demand for sexual intercourse. She's not ready for that; she may not be ready for that even until she's married. So she "backs off."

But that doesn't mean she doesn't like you. She may like you very much. She may even feel in love with you. But feeling that you like or love each other doesn't necessarily mean that you're ready for sex.

So if she (or he) backs off, respect the feelings. Don't push!

I would like to know how you come on to a girl. Do you act polite? *—Sixth-grade boy.*

As I've said, there's no one way for people to relate to each other. Just get to know each other really well before you "come on." And *yes*, always act polite. That doesn't mean you have to act stiff and formal. Real politeness is being kind to another person, finding out how that person feels, and considering the person's feelings. You can have a lot of fun and laughter and liveliness together and still be polite!

How long does it take to get a girl hot? *—Fifth-grade boy.*

A lot of boys asked questions like this. The answer is that it's the wrong question! A girl (or woman) isn't a machine. You don't say words X, Y, and Q, push buttons 3 and 4, rub areas 14 and D, and then in 3½ minutes she's "hot." A girl is a person, and the most important thing for her, and for all people, is to be treated like a person, with feelings and knowledge and ideas about what's right and wrong.

There are lots of things that cause girls and women to become sexually excited—what they see, hear, feel, think. Earlier in this book, I've written about some of these things. But it's not simply a matter of machinery and body parts.

If you really like somebody and you don't want to have sex or kiss or anything, but you like him, how do you say no? Will he hate you and never love you anymore? —*Sixth-grade girl.*

You can just explain your feelings: "Look, I really do like you. I like doing things with you. But I just don't want to do sexy things. I don't even feel ready to kiss you—or anybody else except my family. I'm just not ready to do sexy stuff. OK?"

If a boy doesn't understand that, if he doesn't respect your desires, then it means he really doesn't love you. He may be sexually attracted to you, but if he loved you, then he'd respect *all* of you, including your feelings.

If you think a boy is likely to "try something" if you go somewhere with him, decide *in advance* what you will do and won't do. And then talk about it. If you talk, he may not even put you in a spot where you have to say *no*, because he will understand and not try.

Also, try to explain how you feel in a kind way. Don't make him feel he's bad or nasty—unless he tries to force you. That *is* bad and nasty, and you don't have to be gentle in telling him so and getting away from him.

The main thing, for boys *and* girls, is to keep explaining your feelings to each other, whatever they are. That way, you can enjoy being together, together in things that are serious and things that are just fun.

—5—

Families

What is a family anyway? How do you know if you're in a family? *—Sixth-grade boy.*

A family is usually described as a mother and a father and some children who live in a house or apartment called *home.* Some families may have only one parent; other families include grandparents or other people. The family is the oldest human institution. It's the basic unit of human life together—all over the world.

Most people will belong to two families in their lifetime—the one they were born into, and the one they will create when they grow up and get married.

A typical family has two main purposes. One is to allow a man and woman—husband and wife—to live together in a way that people approve of, in a marriage. They enjoy companionship and sexual life together. The other purpose is for them to have children, to have a place where the chidren are protected, brought up, and trained until they are mature enough to leave and be on their own.

At its best, a family provides steady love and care for all its members, no matter what. (Unfortunately, not all families do this.)

So, "how do you know if you're in a family?" You look around at the people you live with and see whether they, including you, do what I've just explained.

Some pretty strange combos call themselves families these days. Are they families? *—Fourth-grade boy.*

Any two or more people who choose to live together and help and care for each other are a family. It could be any combination of

93

relatives—maybe a grandmother, her daughter, her two children, an uncle, and a cousin from out of town. It could be a young unmarried mother and her child or children (though that's often a tough situation). It could be grandparents and their grandchildren, with no parents of the children. Even a couple of grandparents, whose children have all grown up and left, are still a family. The main thing is that family members live together and provide each other with housing, protection, and care.

It's interesting that only about one-third of American families today are so-called "typical families," with a mother and a father and child or children living together in a home.

When I think of family, I think of a whole bunch of people all over the place. They're my relatives. Isn't that a family? —*Sixth-grade girl.*

Yes, it is. It's called an *extended family.* Lots of extended families keep in touch with each other by visiting, telephoning and writing letters. Sometimes they organize a reunion of as many people in the extended family as can come. That often gives family members a wonderful feeling of loving and caring for lots of people, and having those people care about them too.

A great many boys and girls asked questions and gave opinions about young girls having children:

A young girl I know had a baby. She was in ninth grade. Is that a family? She lives with her mother. Her boyfriend doesn't even come around. Is that a friend? —*Fifth-grade boy.*
What do you need to raise a baby besides diapers? Is it harder than it looks to raise a family? (A friend of mine in another school is pregnant and nobody knows.) —*Fourth-grade girl.*

Maybe a good way to start answering these questions is to quote what another fourth-grade girl wrote: "People think sex is making love and having children, but raising a family is harder than that. You have to first get a job, to buy the house, food, clothes, and pay bills. Teens don't do it like that. The way they do it is so hard sometimes they have to kill the children."

In fact, they rarely kill their children, but it *is* very hard for a young girl who is really still a child herself to care for and bring up a child. Somebody called it "kids having kids," and it doesn't work very well. It doesn't make for very good families. Often a kid with a kid gets very angry and tired and takes it out on the baby. Such babies are called *battered children* because they are abused by their parents.

The Reverend Jesse Jackson once said, "It's easy to *become* a father or *become* a mother. But it takes a real man or a real woman to *be* a good father or *be* a good mother."

So the boy's and girl's questions above are good ones. A ninth-grade mother living with *her* mother is a family, but probably a very difficult one for the ninth-grader to raise a child well. And obviously it takes a lot more than diapers to raise a baby.

Yes, to raise a family is harder than it looks. That's a big reason why boys and girls should think hard and talk together a lot before they have sex. (See again the questions on whether you're ready for sex, on pages 60–61.)

Who in the family really takes charge, woman or man? —*Fifth-grade boy.*
Should someone really be boss, or is it better to work things out? And why can't I help with decisions? —*Sixth-grade girl.*

There's no way to answer these questions. It's different in every family. The traditional way is for the father to be the head of the family—to make the big decisions and "settle" arguments, to "take charge." That works in many families. But nowadays wives and husbands do much more sharing of problems and jobs and decisions than they used to.

A famous old joke is about the happily married husband who said, "When my wife and I got married, we agreed that she'd decide all the small questions and I'd decide the big questions. So far, after fifteen years, there haven't been any big questions."

I think there's no doubt that it's better to "work things out" together than to have a "boss," but many husbands seem to have to *feel* as if they are boss, and their wives are sensible enough to let them feel that way.

As for the children taking part in making decisions, it's a good idea. The older the children are, the more things they should be able to decide or help decide. Obviously, you wouldn't ask a four-year-old to help decide questions like "Do we need a new roof on the house?" or "What kind of stove should we get?" or "Should we move to the house in the next block?" But four-year-olds *could* help decide how they'd like to arrange things in their room or what would be good to have for supper tonight.

On the other hand, most older children and teenagers are ready and able to help decide lots of questions about family life— all the way from painting a room to how the family spends its time. Perhaps the best way to start taking part in family decisions is to earn the right. How? Not by demanding it, but by giving intelligent opinions and needed information that show you are good at deciding.

Why can't we just make our own decisions and run our lives, instead of having our families do it for us? Why don't they give us a chance to grow up? Why do they treat us as if we were still babies? *—Fifth-grade girl.*

Preteens haven't got enough experience to "run their own lives" entirely. They need some rules and guidance. They still need the protection and security of a home and family. Among the things they need are food, house, protection from danger, transportation, advice, and love. They also need rules about what they are allowed to do. For example, a fifth-grade boy would need to know that he has to go to school; to tell his parents where he is going to be when he's away from home; to agree to rules about behavior if he's going to have friends over to the house; to know what parts of the house he can use; to know what food and supplies he can use, and when.

However, sometimes parents set too many rules. It's quite natural, then, for young people to feel as if they're being "treated like babies." If you feel that way, talk about it with your parents. Find a time when there's no argument going on and ask, "Can we talk about something important?" Then calmly say what decisions you'd like to be able to make for yourself. Also tell what parts of your life you'd like to be able to run more for yourself.

Next, *listen* to what your parents say! Maybe they have good reasons for the rules they have made. If you listen to each other and don't aruge, all of you will understand better.

You might offer to take over responsibility for parts of your life and the family's life. Maybe you could offer to repair some things around the house by a certain date; or cook some meals; or do some regular shopping; or keep the car clean; or whatever else you think you can do that would be useful to the family.

Then, if you show you are responsible and can act more like an adult and less like a "baby," you'll probably be treated more like an adult.

However, rules are important in any family. Young teenagers may even find that sometimes it's useful to be able to tell their friends that they just aren't allowed to do someting. "My parents won't let me!"

One of the best ways to grow up, strong and safely, is to ask for fewer rules and to *show* that you can live responsibly without them. The best way to show it is to do your jobs well. The more you can do well, the fewer rules you'll need. As you grow, you can constantly negotiate for more independence. Then use your independence wisely.

How come families seem to be nicer to guests? What's the point? —*Fifth-grade girl.*

It's just sensible and pleasant to be nice to guests. Families are trying to help the guests have a good time. They won't have a good time if parents and children argue and "act natural" when the guests are there.

But when families are together just with themselves, it's much better to be able to act natural most of the time. That doesn't mean acting nasty, but it means feeling pretty free to say what you want. Often, an argument is a very good way for families to understand each other. And when the argument is over, everybody feels better—maybe not right away, but later, when they think it over. If you feel very bad after an argument, try to find a time later, when you've cooled off, to talk about it calmly.

You wouldn't want to be treated like a guest in your own house, would you?

How do you know if your family really loves you? Do you guess? —*Sixth-grade girl.*

It's almost certain your family does love you! But that doesn't mean they always act that way. In most families, people get angry at each other now and then. And in many families, people don't remember to *say* what they *feel*; they forget to say, "I love you," or to give a squeeze or hug or kiss or pat on the back to *show* it.

So if you wonder, for example, whether your father loves you, ask him, "Gee, Dad, do you really love me?" He'll probably be amazed at the question. "Of course I do!" he may say, or "What do you mean? You know I love you." Then you can say what it is that makes you wonder if he loves you. You might say, "But you're always yelling at me." Or "You never say you do." Or "I don't think you act as if you love me." That may get you into a good talk. Both of you will learn from it. And one of the things you both may learn is to say and show that you love each other. That means *you* have to say it and show it as well as your father (or your mother or brother or sister).

Who is usually more loving, mother or father?   —*Fourth-grade girl*.

There's no way to answer this for all families. Usually both mothers and fathers love their children more than anything. But it's a fact that in many families mothers find it easier to show and talk about love than fathers do. Therefore, they seem more loving. It has to do mostly with the way girls and boys are brought up. Many girls are told and shown that it's OK to cry, to act affectionate, and to hug and kiss each other and other people. It's the way they're supposed to grow up to be women—and mothers. But many boys are told and shown that that's not the way boys are supposed to behave. It's "girlish" or "sissy" for them to cry when they're not babies anymore. They don't hug or kiss very much.

So mothers quite often seem more loving than fathers. But that doesn't mean fathers love you less. They just have a harder time showing it.

How come some people don't even care how their children feel?   —*Fifth-grade girl*.

Many parents *seem* not to care, because they have so many other things to do and worry about. They've got their jobs to worry about; they have to run the house. Maybe they worry about their relatives or friends outside the house, people in the neighborhood. And they have to pay attention to them, not just their own kids.

Then there are other parents who have so many difficult feelings of their own that they have a hard time understanding how their children feel. Often parents may yell at a child, "I don't care how you feel! Just do what I tell you!" When a parent sounds like that, you'd better try to do what you're told.

But then it's your job to find a way to let your parents know how you feel. Maybe you'll get angry and they'll know. Maybe you'll cry and they'll know. Maybe you'll slam a door, or look very sad, or say, "You just don't care how I feel!" and they'll know. Try to find a time to talk. You could say, "Mom, I need to talk about how I feel." If she's too busy, say it again and ask, "When can we talk?" You can even ask, "Don't you even *care* how I feel?" Talk to your dad, too.

Almost all parents do care how their children feel. And sometimes children remember to ask their parents how *they* feel. "Gee, Mom (or Dad), how do you feel about that?" That's a good way to start sharing feelings.

As I get older, I'm beginning to discover how different and loving my parents are. Why am I finding this out so late? —*Sixth-grade boy*.

What a wonderful discovery for a sixth-grade boy—or girl! Why so late? It's because when children are young they can't really see very well beyond themselves. They tend to think of their father and mother as figures of authority—FATHER and MOTHER. They seem like people to rely on and obey as *parents*, not complicated individuals with their own interests and problems. Parents are seen as figures who give orders and run things and provide what young children need, including love. But the children may not really *understand* it's love; they just *feel* it. They may not even know they feel it.

But when children get near their teens, their minds have grown enough so that they can see both themselves and their parents as separate, individual people. And they can sort of step back and notice the way their parents act. And it's then that they discover in their minds what they probably already felt: that their parents are "different" individuals and that they are loving.

How do you get your parents to explain better about sex and love and stuff like that? —*Fifth-grade girl*.

Many parents are embarrassed to talk with their children about sex and love. Often, when I speak to groups of parents, mothers and fathers will ask me, "How can we get our children to ask questions?" So, you see, parents often wait and hope for questions from you.

Therefore, get up your courage and ask what you want to know about sex and love and "stuff like that." And when your parents answer, try not to say anthing like "Gee, I already know all that! Do you think I'm a baby or something?" Instead, if you don't get the answers you want, keep asking. After a while, you and your parents may get to be more comfortable talking about love and sex. Remember, people get into trouble because of ignorance, not because of knowledge. What you know won't hurt you. What you *don't* know may hurt you.

I think it's good to have sex education in school because then you can get your parents talking. What do you think? —*Fifth-grade boy*.

I agree that it's good to have sex education in school for boys and girls your age. There are two reasons. One is that at school you can get correct information and a chance to discuss it with your classmates and teachers. The other reason is that it gives you an opening to talk with your parents, just as the question suggests. If you have sex education at school, do talk about it at home, too. Learn what your parents' ideas are. Learn what they think is right and wrong. That will help you develop your own ideas about right and wrong.

When I'm older and have kids, what should I say when they ask where babies come from? Should I tell them the truth or should I wait till they are about nine years old? —*Fourth-grade girl*.

I was surprised that quite a few girls, and some boys, asked what to tell *their* children when the time comes. My answer is:

Parents should answer all the questions their children ask, no matter what the children's age. They should tell them the truth. There's no need to wait till age nine, or any other specific age. Certainly by age five or six it's good for children to know some facts, simply explained—something like this:

"Babies begin when a father and mother mate. They lie down together. The father places his penis in the mother's vagina. It is a very pleasant thing for both of them to do, making love. After a little while sperms come out of the father's penis. They swim up inside the mother, and there they meet a tiny egg. One sperm joins the egg. Then the fertilized egg grows in the uterus (*not in the stomach*). The uterus is a special place where the egg gets its food through a special tube. After about nine months, the fertilized egg has grown into a baby, and it's ready to be born. Then the mother's uterus pushes the baby out through her vagina, the same opening the sperms went in. That's the way babies are made.*

What age should I ask to know about the birds and the bees? Should it be thirteen?   —*Sixth-grade boy.*

You should ask now. It would have been good if you had asked, or your parents had told you, when you were much younger.

Another sixth-grade boy wrote, "In my family, we talk about sex openly. If anybody has questions, we just ask. Words describing genitals are OK, except slang ones. I think children with this kind of childhood are lucky children." Right!

It's pretty hard for me to keep a straight face when I talk to my parents about sex. It's a lot easier to talk to my friends. Why?
—*Sixth-grade boy.*

In our society, it's quite common for parents and children to get embarrassed when they try to talk together about sex. It is such a personal subject, both for the parents and the children. That's true; it does have a personal side. But information about sex isn't personal. So you can start talking about information. And then maybe later you'll feel comfortable talking about your ideas and

*Two very good books with pictures to help explain this are: *How Babies Are Made*, by Andrew Andry and Steven Schepp (New York: Time-Life, 1968); and *Making Babies*, by Sara Bonnett Stein (New York: Walker, 1974).

feelings. (Sometimes it can be a help to use a book like this one. Pick out some of the questions in the book and talk about them.)

Some, but not all, boys and girls find it easier to talk with their friends. Fine, go ahead and talk. The only trouble is that people your own age often don't have the correct information. So you exchange rumors and things that aren't true. Again, it can be helpful to have a book to share.

One reason it is good to learn to talk comfortably about sex is that when you begin to have dates, and to fall in love, and eventually when you marry, it's a great advantage to be able to talk with your partner about sex. There are lots of couples, married and unmarried, who'd be much happier if they had learned to talk about sex when they were young.

I haven't gotten my period yet, but when I do, who can I tell? My parents never talk to me about anything like sex or getting your period. My whole family's like that.   —*Sixth-grade girl*.

A great many families are like that. But why not try saying someting like "Mom, I've got to talk to you about something important. It's personal. When can we talk?" I'm sure she'd be glad to talk. She probably wishes *you* would talk!

If you just can't talk to your mother or father, you should talk with someone. Try the school nurse. You do need a person—in addition to a book—to get information from and also get the tampons or pads you will need. If the school nurse can't do it, find a relative you trust, or an older girl who is sensible. Or ask your teacher whom you should talk to.

Are my parents scared of sex? After all, they had me and my two brothers.   —*Fourth-grade girl*.

Probably they're not scared of it. And undoubtedly they had sex more than three times, once for each child! They are scared, or embarrassed, to talk about it. I've already suggested ways to help get started. Try to be brave and help your parents.

My dad tells me I should always tell the truth, but when I think of what he might do to me, I may forget that idea. What would you do?   —*Sixth-grade girl*.

It's best to tell the truth.

That's easy for me to say and obviously hard for the sixth-grade girl to do. There are some things to keep in mind when you need to tell a difficult truth. One is to *whom* you should tell the truth. Another is *when* to tell it. And a third is *how* to tell it.

Let's take an example of a teenage girl—we'll call her Melissa. Suppose Melissa had sexual intercourse with a boy a few days ago. She feels bad about it now. She knows she's too young. She needs to talk, to ask advice. She might even be pregnant. She doesn't know. However, her father has said to her several times, "If I ever hear that you're going around having sex the way these kids are doing these days, I'll really beat some sense into you. I'm not going to have my daughter being a whore!"

And suppose, too, that her father does indeed beat his children when they do things he considers bad and that he's told them not to do. What should Melissa do about telling her truth?

To whom? It probably would be best for Melissa to tell her mother, even though she knows her mother will tell her father. Or she might try to find a time when she could tell them together so that her father won't think she's going behind his back.

When? Melissa should certainly tell her truth when things around the house are calm and when there will be enough time really to discuss things. It wouldn't be good to do it when somebody is rushing off somewhere. It shouldn't be done when it will come as a sudden surprise and shock. Being suddenly surprised and shocked makes a lot of people angry, and then they feel like hitting.

How? If you have a serious problem about something you've done, say so in advance. Say, "Mom and Dad, I've really got a problem." That's a way to make people feel less angry toward you, to make them feel like helping, not scolding or hitting. But if you say something like "OK, here's what I did. So what are you going to do about it?" you'll probably get an angry response.

Another truth Melissa might want to tell her father is how afraid she feels of him, and how she's scared he'll hit her. If she can tell him that calmly, he may understand more and feel less angry. He may even be surprised. Maybe *his* parents hit him when he was young and he thinks that's just the way it is and should be.

If boys and girls—and parents, too—make a habit of telling the truth to each other, in almost every case they will come closer together and understand each other better. So try to tell the truth—to the best person, at the best time, and in the best way—and then take the consequences. Usually they'll be good consequences. When people who live together tell each other lies, or don't tell the truth, it usually leads to bad consequences.

Why are girls and boys afraid to tell their parents they went to bed? I wouldn't be afraid because I know my mom would help me. —*Fifth-grade girl*.

I've already answered this question, I think. But just remember—like this girl, you should know that your mom will help you. Or your dad. Just think carefully when and how you tell.

But if you are sure your parents won't help you, then do find somebody wise, somebody you trust, and tell that person. You need help!

It seems to me that I am growing apart from my mother. It used to be that we would play board games and share our feelings with each other. But now I find myself turning to my father instead. Why is this? —*Sixth-grade boy*.

When you start really growing up, you do grow apart from your parents. After all, you're not going to live with them forever. A job of growing up is to grow more independent.

This is especially true of boys and their mothers, just like the boy who asked the question. They slowly begin to feel that they need to be more separate from their mothers. So it's natural to turn to their fathers. It helps make them feel more like the men they are growing up to be.

When a boy is very young, he probably spends much more time with his mother than with his father. In most families, his mother is *there*; his father isn't. Or, if he goes to a day-care center because his mother has a job, he's usually with women. But there comes a time when he wants to share feelings and problems and questions with men. It's a healthy, natural feeling.

But it doesn't mean there will be no more contact with Mom! It's only growing to be more independent.

How do I explain to my parents and grandparents about dates with girls, R-rated movies, etc., without them saying I'm too young? *—Sixth-grade boy.*

The answer is in the question: *Explain*. That means you have to figure out whether you *are* too young. How old should you be to have dates with girls (or girls to have dates with boys)? Why do parents and grandparents think R-rated movies are bad for you?

So you explain. Then your parents may explain what they think. When they explain, *listen*! If you and your parents both explain and listen, maybe you will agree. Your parents may be right. Parents often are. But they need to hear your ideas. Also, you need to know that in a real family, if you can't agree, then the children have to obey, to do what they're told to. Otherwise, the family might fall apart, because you aren't old and wise enough to run things. So keep on (1) explaining; (2) listening.

What should you do when you do something wrong but there was a good explanation, but your parents won't listen to you? *—Fourth-grade girl.*

First, remember that everybody does wrong things sometimes. Second, parents are sometimes so busy, or so full of their own ideas, that they won't listen. It's that way in most families. So, third, if they won't listen, just say something like "Well, there's a good explanation why I did that! When can I tell it to you?" The chances are they'll find time to hear you.

I'd like to know how to tell my parents I really like girls. But I'd be embarrassed to tell them that. How do I tell them? *—Sixth-grade boy.*

Just work up your courage and tell them! It's important that they know. Of course, for many boys and girls it's embarrassing. But try to find a time to tell them. Once you start telling, it gets easier. And once you tell and explain, then you and your parents can think and plan together so that you can enjoy spending time with girls—or boys, if you're a girl.

How do you go out with a boy without your parents knowing? *—Sixth-grade girl.*

Don't do it! Your parents are responsible for you, and you might need their help. If you very much want to go out with someone and you feel sure your parents wouldn't allow you to, then you need to have a talk with them. Let them know why you want to go out, and listen to their reasons why they're against it. Chances are, if you talk it over well, you can come to a sensible agreement that will be good for all of you. If you can't, keep discussing. Don't sneak. Don't disobey.

My mom and dad fight a lot. I want to know if they are just play fighting or real fighting? —*Fifth-grade girl*.
Sometimes my mom and dad argue and fight, and then I go and say, "Stop fighting," and they they will say, "We aren't fighting." What should I do about this? It gets me sad.   —*Fifth-grade boy*.

When parents fight, often it is a way they communicate with each other. They feel angry, so they express their anger. They shout; they may cry. But often, after the fight, they understand each other better. They have exchanged feelings. So it isn't "play fighting." That is, it's not a game. It's a way of talking. And it isn't exactly "real fighting," which means trying to win a battle against an enemy.

That doesn't mean they don't want to win the argument (or "fight"). They probably do. But in the winning or losing, they probably get to understand each other better. And often, maybe when you don't hear them, they will say, "I'm sorry" or "I didn't mean to get so mad." And one parent may end up doing what the other person wanted done—or stop doing what the other didn't like.

So probably that's why the fifth-grade boy's parents say, "We're not fighting." There's nothing he should try to do about it. Children don't have to settle the arguments of their parents! The arguments are not the children's fault.

And of course it "gets me sad," as the boy said. But when he realizes it's usually a healthy part of life, he may feel less sad. And later on he can say to his parents, "When you fight, it gets me sad." Parents should know how their children feel.

Here are some more comments and questions young people wrote on the subject of parents fighting and how children feel about it. How would you react to what they've said?

When we see our parents argue and yell at each other, why do we sometimes cry and wish we could run away and leave this frightening place? How do parents feel when their child sees them fighting? Do they care, or do they wish they could stop and make their child feel safe? —*Fifth-grade girl.*

What subjects do parents fight about? Do they do it mostly because they had a bad day? How does it affect the chilren? —*Fourth-grade girl.*

You love your parents a little less when they yell—fact or opinion? —*Fifth-grade girl.*

Advice to children in families that have problems: Try to learn not to do anything that might enrage your parent(s) and/or get you in trouble. —Sixth-grade boy.

My mother works as a proprietor, and she is angry more often than she used to be before she had her store. Why? —*Sixth-grade boy.*

About how many parents take out their problems on their children? A lot? —*Sixth-grade girl.*

Nobody can say just how many, but, yes, a lot. When people have problems (and, of course, parents are people), often they feel angry. Their tempers are short. Therefore, when something slightly annoying happens, they tend to get mad quickly. If you, the child, happen to be the one who breaks a dish or doesn't clean up a mess, or turns up the radio too loud, you may get a blast of anger. But it's probably not really meant to be blasted at you. It's just that your parent has worries, and your one little added problem causes anger.

If you can tell when your parents are feeling this way, then it might be well to follow the advice of the sixth-grade boy above who says you should try to avoid doing anything that might make them even a little bit mad during that time.

My dad and mom always get into fights with me and I feel really bad. How do I show them I love them without losing the fight? —*Sixth-grade girl.*

Just remember what the fight was about. It *wasn't* about whether you love them or they love you. It was about your messy room, or their refusing to let you do something, or who gets to watch what TV program when—or whatever. Therefore, when the fight's over, you can't lose any fight by saying, "Well, I love you anyway" or by just giving them a hug.

If they say something like "Well, if you loved me, you'd keep your room neat," that's tough. But keeping your room neat (reasonably) is probably a good idea, so try keeping it neat. Or you can explain *why* you like it messy. But you can also say, "Messy room or neat room, I still love you!" That might get a laugh, and a laugh helps.

If your parents aren't getting along very well and they get into a big fight right in front of you, what should you do?   —*Sixth-grade girl*.

Probaby the best thing to do is to go away quietly to a place where you can't hear the fight. After all, it's their fight.

Many, many boys and girls asked about divorce. Some were children of divorced parents; others were children who feared their parents might get divorced; and others just wanted information.

Why do people get divorced? Are there lots of reasons for it, or just a few, or only one? My mom and dad are not divorced, and if they do get divorced I would be pretty sad and kind of mad. —*Fourth-grade girl*.

My mom and dad got a divorce when I was three years old. I ask my mom why and she always says when I get older she will tell me, and I am tired of her saying that. When will I be older? —*Fifth-grade girl*.

Please give us some facts about divorce in your book. It's a big question for a lot of kids. —*Fifth-grade boy*.

First, why do men and women get divorced? Mainly it's because they can't deal with the problems of being married. They may disagree about money, about where to live, about what they want to do with their lives.

They may have thought they were in love and then found that they didn't really love each other. It was just sexual attraction, and there's a lot more to living together than sex!

They may have different tastes and values—one may want to

go out to parties all the time, while the other thinks marriage means staying at home and being with the family most of the time.

One may get hooked on alcohol or drugs and become impossible to live with, and yet refuse to get treated and cured.

They may hit each other and abuse each other with words until one or both can't bear it any longer.

Or one may be "unfaithful" sexually—that is, have sex with a person outside the marriage. That's called *adultery* (a-DULL-tur-ee).

You see, a divorce can happen for a lot of reasons, and often it happens for a combination of reasons, not just one. In the United States, about half of all marriages end in divorce.

Here are some more facts—or some pretty well-established opinions—about divorce:

Some couples continue to stay married even though they are very unhappy together or even hate each other. I'm talking about unhappiness over a long period of time, not just unhappiness after a bad argument. But such parents are likely to be more harmful to their growing children than if they got divorced and ended everybody's misery.

Parents who get divorced are usually quite sad about it because of the children. Almost always, they do care about what divorce will do to the children. They are also sad that they could not stay happily married. It's a hard thing to bear, but not as hard as living together unhappily.

However, there *are* some selfish parents, or childish parents, who don't love their children. If a parent—and usually it's the father—simply abandons the children, he probably doesn't love them. But this isn't because they aren't lovable. It's because the father (or sometimes mother) doesn't have the ability to love. It's not the children who are the problem; the parent is the problem.

If one of your parents doesn't love you, it's not your fault. I say that again because so many children think it is their fault. Some parents just aren't able to love. But if you feel a parent doesn't love you, you can actually say this to the parent. You may get an answer that will help you. You can also ask if there are some things you do that annoy the parent. If there are, maybe you can work on changing those things.

If you wonder whether your parents might be thinking about a divorce, it's better to ask them. Worrying, and keeping those worries secret, is very hard for children. It's better to know the truth, and it's good to ask your parents to tell you the truth.

Certainly the fifth-grade girl who asked, "When will I be older?"—old enough to know why her parent got divorced—*is* old enough. She should remember that her mother may feel it will be painful to explain about a bad experience, and that there may be parts of it that her mother needs to keep private. But her fifth-grade daughter has a right to a good, understandable answer. Therefore, she could try saying something like "Mom, there's an important question I really need to ask. When can we talk?" It should be a time when neither one is in a hurry or angry.

Another point: It's all right for you to have opinions about the way your parents behave. Parents aren't perfect. You aren't behaving badly because you don't like the way one or both of your parents is acting.

If there is a divorce, the children usually (but not always) stay with their mother. This means that the mother has *custody* (CUSS-tuh-dee). The father gets the right to spend some time with his children, but the law has decided that they will live with their mother. Sometimes the father has custody, and that means that the chilren must live with their father. Occasionally, the parents have *joint custody*. In that case, the law has decided that they may take turns having the children live with them.

Many children hope and hope that their parents will get back together again. Of course, you're free to hope what you want. But the fact is that divorced couples hardly ever do get back together. Therefore, it's better to hope and work for more realistic things.

Divorces happen not because of what the children do. They don't happen because you were bad. *You* can't get your parents back together. Divorces happen because the parents are unhappy with *each other*. The divorce, if it happens, *isn't your fault.*

But just because there is anger in the house doesn't mean there will be a divorce. Even very loving parents feel and act angry sometimes. Anger is a part of human nature. It isn't bad; it isn't a crime. But if there is too much of it, it is a problem. Often, talking about it helps.

If your parents are getting divorced, it's OK to feel sad. It's a very sad thing for a child. It's OK to cry about it. When terrible things are happening, most people need to cry. The hardest thing, probably, is to pretend you don't care, to pretend you're not sad. The truth is better than pretending.

One of the hardest things for children in a divorce is that their parents sometimes engage in a sort of tug-of-war, trying to get the children's love. They may say nasty things about each other, hoping that that will get the children's love. (Perhaps they both want custody but know that only one of them can have the children live with them.) When parents act that way, it's tough! Just knowing that may help.

Do people sometimes get married just for an excuse to have sex? Then, when they get tired of sex with each other, if that's all they have, is that why they get divorced? —*Sixth-grade boy.*

Yes, some people do get married just for sex. But these days, many people have sex before they get married. Sometimes they find that they really don't like being together, and they can separate before marriage without the pain of getting divorced.

Other people find that sex isn't so wonderful when they first get married. But they really love each other, and they learn how to please each other, and sex gets better and better. Still other married people love being married even though having sex isn't a very important part of their marriage. They enjoy other parts of their lives more—doing things together; talking; having children; laughing; having friends; caring for a house; planning for a good life and carrying out the plans.

However, to answer the boy's last question, yes, if sex is all a couple has and they get tired of it, they are likely to get divorced.

Should people wait longer before they get married so they don't get divorced? —*Fifth-grade boy.*

Yes.

A sixth-grade boy wrote some strong words about this: "If you think you might get divorced, why get married in the first place? I mean, that to me is the stupidest thing you could do. If you're going to love somebody, it better be for real. Maybe you'd better go on a camping trip, and get dirty, and get wet, and have some problems. *Then* you might know if it's for real. Am I crazy?"

No, you're very sensible!

Do parents ever think about anybody but themselves when they get into fights or divorced? The kid usually doesn't get to say anything and usually gets neglected. Do parents ever care?
—Fifth-grade girl.

Yes, most fighting and divorcing parents do think about their kids. But they are probably very wrapped up in their own problems. So they forget how the kids feel. That's why it's important for the kids to ask what the truth is, what the situation is. It's important, too, for the kids to express their feelings—for example, to say, "I really feel neglected." If they express that feeling, they'll probably find their parents do care and may remember to show it more.

I feel scared when my parents fight, because every time they do I think they'll get a divorce. I hate divorces. Can you prevent divorces? *—Fifth-grade girl.*

We've already discussed this, but it needs repeating. Most parents fight sometimes. Anger is a part of our nature. Fighting doesn't mean divorce. But lots of fighting may mean trouble. For some couples, though, it is a way of communicating.

No, children cannot prevent divorces. But sometimes the love parents feel for their children helps keep them together and deepens their love for each other. If it doesn't, it's not the children's fault.

How should you take it when your parents get a divorce?
—Sixth-grade girl.

It's not a matter of how you "should" take it. No one can say how another person should feel—you just feel, and that's not your fault. But it's a fact that for most boys and girls, the divorce of their parents is hard to take. One fifth-grade girl asked, "Kids feel kind of split when their parents get divorced—fact or opinion?" The answer is: Usually, yes; it's a fact.

However, in the end it probably will turn out to be not so bad.

There are millions of children of divorced parents who have lived through the shock and unhappiness and are healthy and well and enjoying life. Often, parents remarry. That doesn't mean they will stop loving their children. Usually, their love remains as strong as ever. Also, the new husband or wife, who are stepparents, can love their stepchildren and get great pleasure in having them as part of a new family. Furthermore, the children find that they learn to enjoy both their parents and their stepparents. As one fifth-grade boy wrote, "Any boy or girl whose parents are divorced or remarried ought not to be discouraged or sad, because it really isn't their fault. As a matter of fact, I kind of like my dad and mom being divorced and then my dad being remarried, because it's just one more person to take care of me."

Is it wrong to talk about marriage, divorcing, etc., with people who aren't in or part of your family, even if they are very close friends?   —*Fourth-grade girl*.
My friend's parents are divorced. Sometimes he's happy and stuff like that, but sometimes he's edgy, moping, and sad. How can I make my friend feel better?   —*Fifth-grade boy*.
Boys and girls need very much to have a chance to talk over the problems of their lives, especially deep, tough ones like divorce. So, *no*, it's not wrong to talk about these problems with a close friend. Not only is it not wrong; it is a real service of friendship you can perform. The fifth-grade boy asks, "How can I make my friend feel better?" The answer: By listening and understanding and letting him know you really share how he's feeling. People need a "support system"—people who offer help and sympathy—for a shattering experience like divorce in a family. You can be a part of a friend's support system.

**I want to make my mother happy, and my father. My dad has just been remarried. But when I get home I say to my mother that I hate his new wife. I don't hate her, but she's too "fake" and she's not my mother, but I don't know how to tell my dad that.
—*Fourth-grade girl*.**
This girl has taken on a big job, an impossible job: to make both her divorced mother and divorced father happy. No child, or

anyone else, can do that! All she can do is to try to be a little bit helpful. It's okay to tell your mother she hates her stepmother when she acts "fake." That's a real feeling and she needs to share it. Also, it would be okay for her to tell her dad, too. He probably would want to know, and he might be able to help his new wife understand better how to act toward her stepdaughter.

In most cases, after the shock of divorce, and after all the adjustments, things work out pretty well for the children. But it takes time, talk, and thoughtfulness.

If your parents are divorced, how do you react when they ask which one you want to spend the most time with?   —*Sixth-grade boy*.

If you love both your parents, this is a very hard decision to make. You naturally want to please both your parents and make them happy. But you have to think of yourself. So my answer is: Listen to the question. Then ask for time to think it over. If you can, find some wise person you trust to discuss it with. When you have decided, answer honestly what you think would be best for you. If you can say so truthfully, tell both your parents that you love both of them. That will make both them and you happier, and it will help to ease any hurt feelings.

Why is there rivalry between brothers and sisters? —*Fifth-grade boy*.

Rivalry (RY-vull-ree) means trying to get the same thing someone else has. Or it means trying to be or do something better than someone else. It would be a miracle if brothers and sisters weren't rivals sometimes. It's just natural for people to want things that other people have, or to want to beat out somebody for something.

Brothers and sisters live together in a limited space. Most of them would like more things, or even more love, than they have. Therefore, they are bound to be rivals sometimes. Other times they will be friends and they'll feel family love for each other. If rivalry leads to fighting and a lot of arguing and abuse, it's time for a family talk—all together or one with another. Maybe you can work out plans for sharing instead of being rivals. By the way, brothers and sisters in a family are called *siblings* (SIB-lings), and what we're talking about is *sibling rivalry*. It's a very common condition!

We have a baby girl, but my dad always kisses her. And he used to talk with me about my day. But now, because we have a new baby, and a six-year-old girl, and myself, I feel that this is slowly but surely destroying our family relationships. What should I do? —*Fourth-grade boy.*

Remember that when you were a baby, you got a lot of kissing too. Babies are just very kissable! Your father probably doesn't even know how much you miss talking with him about your day. So tell him! It'll probably make him feel good. And then your baby sister and you won't have to be such rivals for your father's time.

Why do families fight? Every time I walk past my brother, I have the urge to hit him on the back of the head. I don't know why, but my hand just goes without my telling it. —*Sixth-grade boy.*

I've already explained why families fight. As far as your hand goes, why not try attaching your hand to your brain! Don't say, "I'll never hit my brother again." That's probably too big an order. But say, "Okay, brain, you're in control. You're going to force my hand *for one whole day* not to touch my brother." For one day, your brain can probably manage it. Then the next day will be easier. The first thing you know, you'll have broken the brother-head-hitting habit.

How can you deal with your sister who's a punk rocker and is always torturing you about your clothes and hair, and won't leave you alone? —*Sixth-grade girl.*

It's your hair and they're your clothes. Why not just say so? Also, your sister has a right to her way of life (as long as it doesn't mess up other people's lives), and you have a right to yours. So why not talk about it? A good time might even be at the supper table with your parents, when you might all talk about the rights of each family member. You might even make a list of rights, including more than the right not to be tortured about hair and clothes.

—6—

Five Good Guides

In the introduction to this book, I suggested five guides for how to approach matters of love and sex. Well, we've discussed a lot more than just love and sex. I think the five guides are good for all parts of your life. Here they are again:

- Tell the truth.
- Know the facts.
- Don't harm yourself or others.
- Consider the feelings of others.
- Consider your own feelings.

These may seem like very simple ideas. Well, they are simple to write down, but they are often very complicated and difficult to actually follow!

I close this book with a statement from one of the youngest people who answered the questionnaire on people, love, sex, and families. He was a fourth-grader, and he wrote, "Love families and all other people. Respect older people and young children. Be helpful to others. Let someone borrow your things if they ask you for them. Teach somebody what they don't know very well. Play with others if they don't have a playmate. Help your parents when they come home from their job." That's not quite the last word. Think about what you've read in this book. Then, on a sheet of paper, write down a short, clear answer to this question: *What should I do about people, love, sex, and families? How should I act?*

Maybe your parents and a couple of friends, or siblings, might want to try the question, too. Ask them to, and then compare your answers and discuss the ideas in them. Discussion of people, love, sex, and families should never end—it should continue for the rest of your life.

Index

In this book, as I've said, the first time I use and explain a new word, it's printed in *italics*. But as you read on in the book, you may forget what the word means. If you do, look it up in this index. If it's printed in **boldface type**, you'll find it defined in the text on the page numbered also **boldface**. Examples: **species**, **5**; **prejudice**, **8**; **uterus**, **21**.

119